By No Means Equal

Reclaiming the Soul

Also by William Wildblood

Meeting the Masters
978-1-78099-168-9 (Paperback)
978-1-78099-169-6 (ebook)

Remember the Creator
978 1 78535 927-9 (Paperback)
978 1 78535 928-6 (ebook)

Earth Is a School
978 1 78904 791-2 (Paperback)
978 1 78904 792-9 (ebook)

By No Means Equal

Reclaiming the Soul

William Wildblood

AXIS MUNDI
BOOKS

Winchester, UK
Washington, USA

JOHN HUNT PUBLISHING

First published by Axis Mundi Books, 2023
Axis Mundi Books is an imprint of John Hunt Publishing Ltd., 3 East Street, Alresford,
Hampshire SO24 9EE, UK
office@jhpbooks.com
www.johnhuntpublishing.com
www.johnhuntpublishing.com/axismundi-books

For distributor details and how to order please visit the 'Ordering' section on our website.

ISBN: 978 1 80341 348 8
978 1 80341 349 5 (ebook)
Library of Congress Control Number: 2022913908

A CIP catalogue record for this book is available from the British Library.

Design: Lapiz Digital Services

UK: Printed and bound by CPI Group (UK) Ltd, Croydon, CR0 4YY
Printed in North America by CPI GPS partners

We operate a distinctive and ethical publishing philosophy in
all areas of our business, from our global network of authors to
production and worldwide distribution.

Contents

Introduction

All cultures have a defining belief or myth on which they base themselves. In most cases it is a religious one which takes various forms but all of them are rooted in a reality beyond this world. However, that of the contemporary West does not follow the traditional pattern for it derives from a belief in the primacy of matter rather than spirit. The modern myth is egalitarianism, the insistence that all men are equal. This idea blossomed at the time of the French revolution with its rallying cry of *liberté, égalité, fraternité* though the seeds were sown much earlier, going back to certain streams of thought in the medieval period. But, in the sense we understand it today, it is a product of the eighteenth-century Enlightenment.

Egalitarianism did not form a part of traditional Western belief except for the idea that we were all created by the One Father, God. But that doesn't mean we are all equal. The natural order in tradition, not just in the West but more or less everywhere in the world where civilisation has developed, was hierarchical and this reflects the belief that there is a vertical dimension to life. That implies transcendence, the denial of which is virtually the definition of modernity which, with a singular lack of imagination, has reduced reality to the world of appearance or what can be grasped by the senses, ignoring the fact that the senses filter as much as they reveal.

Now, in the twenty-first century we have arrived at a belief in radical equality through the spread of communism for communism, whether we realise it or not, underpins the philosophical assumptions of almost all contemporary thought. Not so much in the overt political or economic sense but culturally speaking it does where it has become deeply embedded since the 1960s. It has reached the point at which to challenge this assumption marks you out as an immoral person.

Communism is atheistic and materialistic. There are occasional rather feeble attempts to dispute this but they fail as they must since communist ideology is entirely concerned with this world and has no sense of a spiritual goal for humanity. Hence, it should not be hard to see that egalitarianism, though it too sometimes claims to have a spiritual basis, is in fact a thoroughly materialistic and atheistic doctrine. This makes sense chronologically since the two came about at the same time. The belief in equality in the form it is held nowadays did not arise from any religious principle but from a rejection of religion and its substitution by a belief system centred on the human being in its earthly form. If you want to associate it with religion you would have to say it took what belongs to the spiritual level and applied it to the material level, in the process abolishing the spiritual or, at the very least, making that secondary to the material.

In this book I will start with a series of essays that examine the modern ideology of equality and show that it is essentially an anti-spiritual doctrine, one that denies the reality of the soul using that word to mean the non-material essence of our individual self. Some of the arguments might appear too simplistic to cover all the complexities of socio-economic and political life but I am looking at the question from a metaphysical point of view here, and ultimately everything is downstream from metaphysics anyway. Whether this ideology has arisen now as a natural outcome of humanity reaching a stage in its growth roughly analogous to adolescence when it throws off outer (transcendent) authority and tries to go it alone or whether it is a well-meaning attempt to create a morality in a materialistic society with no higher values or whether it has been put through by forces antithetical to spiritual development specifically to derail higher values, for when everything is equal there is a strong tendency to revert to the lowest common denominator, I shall leave the reader to decide as we go along.

Then we shall proceed to looking at ways in which the egalitarian ethos has affected and corrupted the spiritual search. For it undoubtedly has. Religion is not democratic any more than science or art are but in many instances it is being made so. Misunderstanding the true idea that God is within all of us, we fall into the trap of thinking that he is equally within all of us. Even if that were true, he does not manifest equally in all of us. Like all heresies, if you can call it that, egalitarian ideology takes a piece of the truth and exaggerates its importance while minimising the significance of other aspects of truth. Truths that apply on the level of the One do not apply on that of the Many, and certainly not to the Many as the Many. The Absolute and the Relative are both part of the totality of life but they are different and should not be confused.

There is occasional reference in these pages to the Masters. For more on that subject please see my books *Meeting the Masters* and *Earth Is a School*.

Part I

Liberty and Equality

Equality is the great dogma on which modern liberal Western democracies are built. Nowadays when we talk about Western values this is a large part of what we mean. It was certainly not a traditional Western value. The idea might have seemed like a step forward at a time when the gap between rich and poor, powerful and weak, was as great as it was, and the movement towards less inequality surely did right some wrongs and bring about some benefits in the short term. But the flaw that lies at its heart is now being revealed. If equality, and equality above all, is taken as the foundation of a culture then that culture will collapse to what is attainable by everyone and it will eventually collapse altogether. Equality is contrary to human nature and to enforce it is to force human beings to live against both their natural and their spiritual instincts. It becomes a tool to push the higher down to the level of the lower. This does not mean that the higher should dominate the lower (other than spiritually, it should do that), but liberty and equality are not natural bedfellows despite what the idealists of the Enlightenment might have hoped, and it is liberty that is the great spiritual quality as far as human beings are concerned.

Equality is sometimes said to be rooted in Christianity. If it were how strange it is that it is never mentioned in the Bible and was only discovered to be a Christian virtue 1800 years after the time of Christ. Fellowship in Christ is a Christian virtue but that is not equality which is a materialistic distortion of it. In fact, equality is not a spiritual thing at all for it is actually a property of unformed matter, matter untouched by the creative breath of spirit, which is why you see it most at lower levels of evolution. The more life evolves, the more unequal it becomes because the freer it becomes and yet within that inequality there is also a spiritual oneness. To realise the truth of this apparent paradox is one of the major goals of the spiritual path. It and it alone explains the mystery of love.

Consider this. Where is equality most to be found? Where is it an indisputable reality? It is only fully present in the *prima materia*. In other words, it only exists in nothingness, non-being. The act of creation breaks equality which can only be restored by a levelling back down to the state of chaos, by the destruction of what has been created. Equality can only naturally be present in complete oneness where no difference exists at all. Introduce difference and you banish equality.

Once you grasp this obvious fact it becomes apparent that equality is promoted, whether its advocates are aware of this or not, by something that has an agenda of spiritual destruction. Anything high or noble or great will be destroyed in the push for more equality.

The fact that equality exists at the lowest of levels leads to the fallacious view that we should get back to it as that was when we were supposedly purer and more in harmony with the essence of life. But this is the very opposite of the truth. We should eventually return to the source, i.e., God, but it must be with the fully developed fruits of the journey. Otherwise, what's the point of the journey, indeed of creation itself?

Spiritual understanding shows us that there is an anti-God power in the universe. This is not something that exists independently of God but something given existence by God that has rebelled against him because of the always possible by virtue of what it is misuse of free will. This power wants to undo creation and return it to darkness. Anything good, beautiful or true has necessarily grown out of the inchoate chaos of primeval equality. Satan, to give this power its most recognised name, wants to chop all that down and send it back to nothingness. It is freedom that has given Satan the power to act like this but it is also freedom he wants to destroy because he wants to reduce other beings to spiritual slavery. And the doctrine of equality is a means for doing this because it is profoundly anti-individual.

It is a common belief that to be spiritual requires the loss of individuality. However, we need to understand that God is a God of individuals because he is a God of love, and there is no love without the individual. The attempt to destroy or deny the self, common to some forms of spirituality, is misconceived. It is not the self that should be destroyed, even if that were possible. It is the false self that has separated itself from its source in God and set itself up as independent that must go. But there is also the true self which is where our freedom, which is real, resides. Selves are not equal because they are different and unique but they share a divine source so there is a bond of unity between them. This unity is real but to see souls in terms of equality is to impose a quantitative view onto something spiritual and qualitative. Equality is materialism by another name.

No Rational Basis for Equality

If you believe in God and think that God exists in everyone, you must also see that not everyone reflects the reality of what God is to the same degree. For all people may be manifestations of God, as in they are created by him and have him in them, but clearly none are perfect manifestations which means there are greater and lesser manifestations.

If you don't believe in God but think that we all have some kind of universal spiritual component within us then you must still accept that our awareness and understanding of it differ hugely. As does our ability to express it.

And if you are a materialist then you believe that nothing has real meaning or value anyway unless that be artificially invented by us, so equality is a redundant concept. It's merely an ideological abstraction, an aspiration without real substance. If a materialist wants to say that we all have equal value then that value, according to his scheme of things, is precisely nothing. We are all equal, but equally worthless.

Equality as a real thing rather than a vague abstraction is only possible in something like an ant colony. It would demand the complete abolition of individuality.

It is a perversion of a spiritual truth, namely that God exists in every human being, each one of whom, by virtue of that fact, has the potential to awaken spiritually and become godlike themselves. But we are all at different stages of that journey and some will never reach the destination because it depends on actively wanting to and not all of us do want this. Moreover, even if and when the destination is reached, we will not be equal because we all express our spiritual realisation in individual ways.

Equality is a one-dimensional view of the world which collapses reality to the horizontal, the material level, ignoring the vertical axis of soul. The concept should be rejected and replaced with ideas of justice and fairness wherever these are appropriate. That is because to keep equality in any form whatsoever inevitably reinforces the notion of equality pure and simple as an absolute.

How did this idea ever come about when it is so contrary to reason? One can only assume that in its modern form it is a misunderstanding of Christian teaching, basing itself on the idea that all human beings have the divine within them and, in that sense, all have value and divine potential. God created the human soul and each soul is worthy of respect as an authentic, unique spiritual being. But to go from that to a belief in equality here and now in this mortal world is a non sequitur. The Masters said that **men are by no means equal on the earth plane**. They meant by this that we are free and individual. Quite clearly, they did not intend it as justification for the more evolved, as they put it, to exploit the less so but were simply pointing to the fact that there are more and less evolved people in the world and not to recognise this is not to recognise reality. It is not inequality that is wrong but egotistical reaction to the fact of inequality.

Proponents of the equality idea might claim that without it the door is open for exploitation of the weak by the strong, but that is akin to saying that the idea may be false but it can have good results or that the means justify the ends which is an axiom any schoolchild should know to be false since a cause and its effect cannot be separated. There are other ways of preventing the abuse of a truth than by propagating a lie. Besides, this exploitation would only occur when the belief in human inequality was interpreted without the corresponding belief in God. The problem is not inequality but inequality seen through the lens of atheism or a false spiritual belief as in one voided of love. In all cases, the solution is a correct spiritual understanding that sees the presence of God in all human beings with that presence existing as a potential that needs to be developed.

Equality is contrary to the proper understanding of God because, by limiting everything to the same level, it destroys the sense of hierarchy and transcendence. This means that God is reduced in mystery and majesty. Eventually, if you believe in equality, you will believe yourself to be equal to God. And that means you won't believe in God. But without God, as we should be able to see quite clearly at this stage in the twenty-first century, there is only nihilism and despair, kept at bay by the stimulation of constant entertainment whether that be of the popular variety or the intellectual. Equality, far from being a spiritual belief as it is often conceived of nowadays, is the product of an anti-spiritual materialism.

Once again we see that when humanity abandons belief in a transcendent reality it loses itself in invented substitutions that lead it ever further into illusion. And the end result of living in illusion is invariably spiritual disaster. This all stems from the replacement of true religion with the worship by humanity of itself and the failure to understand that if humanity does not look beyond itself for its true fulfilment it will sink into something less than itself. Egalitarianism really amounts to the promotion of quantity to a universal good with the concomitant demotion of quality as the primary and fundamental factor distinguishing the human soul.

We Are All One

It is a popular and almost unquestioned truism of modern spirituality that everything is one. We are all connected, all brothers and sisters in the great family of humanity with a deep unity that ultimately overrides all other considerations. All differences melt away in the face of oneness. I went along with this idea myself at one time because it seems almost self-evident in an underlying spiritual sense. After all, there's only one God, one Creator. I had reservations but took it as broadly true. To deny it seemed to deny the reality that spirit underlies everything. Therefore, it must be true.

But what if it's not true or, at least, not as true as it is taken to be? To begin with, from a Christian perspective we are all one in Christ but for that to be the case we have to accept Christ. We are not all one outside Christ and even if you extend this to a more universal plane to mean we are all one in God then we surely still have to accept the reality and truth and meaning and fact of God? We have to respond to God within us and do so on a spiritual rather than a mere intellectual or emotional plane. Only then can we meet in a real unity.

Then there are good grounds for thinking that the present time is not one of unity but of separation, of dividing the sheep from the goats. Jesus said he did not come to bring peace (unity) but a sword (division). This is often ignored by those who wish to paint a picture of a false Jesus who loves humanity in its fallen state more than he loves God. Of course, Jesus does love humanity, even fallen, sinful humanity, but he does not love the fallen state and he wants to redeem us from that state and bring us to the reality of God. But for that to happen we must repent our sinful nature. Yes, our sinful nature. We cannot continue in the worldly path and expect God's love to operate regardless. God may love all human beings but above all he loves truth and he loves those more who reflect his own truth back to him.

The modern world demands that we accept everyone on his or her own terms. We are all one regardless of what we are, but this elevates quantity above quality. It is totally at odds with the true spiritual attitude which reverses that hierarchy and sees that what you are is much more important than the basic fact that you are. Spiritual unity can only come about at a higher level and to know this unity you have to fit yourself for that level which means respond to spirit. The material world is not the world of unity but of separation and to force unity onto it on its own level and according to its own terms is to create a lie. No wonder that agenda is being pushed so hard in this day and age when spiritual truth is being parodied and reinterpreted in material terms to deflect us from the hard (for the ego) facts of reality.

There is another point to take into consideration on this matter of oneness. Evolution is a growing out from sameness to difference. We become more individual as we evolve not less so. Insects are a lower form of life than animals, and the higher animals show more individuality than the lower ones. Then when you get to the human kingdom you have real individuals. This no doubt continues. The glory of the saints is that they are so individual, all one in God but fully themselves too. And there is no one in the history of humanity more individual than Christ which is partly why the force of his personality persists through the centuries. He is not a cardboard cut-out saviour but a wholly unique person, just as we all are and we will become more so as we progress into the heart of God. That journey brings out our uniqueness. It does not obliterate it in some faceless uniformity or tasteless spiritual porridge. The very fact of love proves this. You can't have love in oneness, not real love of the sort that lays down its life for its friends. Love needs some degree of separation. In a certain sense, it is the overcoming of oneness and the dismissal of equality.

But still the belief in oneness as the essence of spirituality persists. It is so alluring precisely because it is founded on a truth which is the oneness of God. There is a saying in India that to the enlightened person a stone is the same as a lump of gold. Such a person sees God everywhere and to him everything is God and equally so. There is nothing but God. Oneness. Now, on the face of it this might seem profound but it is actually quite trite. That doesn't stop it being a commonly held opinion among those who turn to certain mystical forms of spirituality after reacting against the materialism or decaying religion of their upbringing. This may be because while the saying, as it stands, is incorrect, there is an element of truth in it. However, it is one that needs to be understood in a somewhat different way to that implied if the statement that a stone and a lump of gold are the same to the wise is taken literally.

For although both may contain the presence of God, they are by no means the same. The truth in the statement is that everything, all of nature, all of existence, shines with the glory of the Lord for those who have eyes to see. But this is not to be understood in a pantheistic sense. God may be in nature but he is not nature. He stands above his creation in his true being even if his presence informs it and holds it together. Perhaps the clue is in the word creation. God and his creation are not the same but God is present in his creation as he must be in anything for it to have existence. If his presence were withdrawn from something then that thing would simply cease to be.

Therefore, God is present in everything as its being but, in himself, he remains transcendent. Moreover, he is present in things to a different degree depending on their nearness, in the sense of correspondence to his true nature, to beauty, to goodness, to him. Let me quote from the Masters here. They said that **beauty is everywhere. It varies in degree according to its closeness to God but there is God in everything and that means beauty**. Now, this statement can be understood as saying that God is in everything but each thing only reflects God according to the degree of its openness to him. In other words, the degree to which it expresses his qualities or has unfolded them from within itself. So a stone is not the same as a lump of gold because it does not reflect God as much as the gold does even though God's presence informs them both.

In like manner, God is in the sinner just as he is in the saint but the saint reveals more of God because he has developed more of his divine nature. However, in this case there is the additional factor that the sinner, unlike the stone, is gifted with free will, and he has not only failed to develop his divine nature, he has also corrupted that with negative qualities that do not come from God, and these are a kind of minus that result in a loss of God. God is still present in the sinner but if the sinner denies or rejects God that presence is diminished. He is then deliberately seeking God's absence and this means he is moving further and further away from God and will eventually, if he does not turn around through contrition or repentance, reach the point where God is not. This is the definition of Hell.

Of course, there can be nowhere where God truly is not but the sinner at this point has so isolated himself by rejection of God that he has reached a condition of total remoteness from God's presence in which the only remaining indication of God is existence itself. He still exists but he has turned his consciousness to stone.

A better understanding of life comes when we acknowledge the foundational fact of unity but also see that in terms of creation the twin principles of unity and hierarchy coexist. Life is being and becoming together not either one alone. Illusions arise when we over-emphasise one part of the whole at the expense of the other. Life is only known when it is expressed and when it is expressed it must take a form. Not only are no two forms the same but the whole point of manifested life is that it grows into ever greater awareness and perfection. If things grow, how can they be the same? How can they be equal? Growth is the denial of oneness. It refutes equality.

Quality and Equality

The great modern drive by the fallen angels who are at war against God is to replace quality with equality. In this way they aim to reduce humanity to a controllable and conformist mass, cut off from any higher understanding than the materialistic. This is why such things as racism and sexism have become the equivalents of secular mortal sins. Anything that offends the idea of equality and oneness must be shown to be evil. No one can be allowed to live outside the fold or, if they do, they must be totally shunned. Today if somebody is branded a racist he is effectively the lowest of the low, and we all live in fear that we may make a mistake and end up condemned.

By the standards of the modern ideology I am a racist because I believe there are differences between ethnic groups which have been separated in evolutionary terms for thousands of years. If evolution has any reality how can that not be the case? This is not even bringing into consideration any what, for want of a better term, we might call occult factors which have to do with different spiritual origins of souls. It is beside the point to say we are all one and these differences don't matter. Of course we are all one and of course the differences don't affect the fundamental brotherhood of man. All life is one in essence but it is hugely varied in expression. There is no absolute equality anywhere. It is certainly a mistake to over-emphasise the differences at the expense of the unity, as has happened in the past, but it is also a mistake to do the opposite as we do nowadays, and over-emphasise the unity at the expense of the differences. The truth is not one or the other but both together, and if both are not respected then disharmony will be the result.

By modern standards I am also a sexist because I believe there are differences between men and women that go much deeper than basic physical biology. The biology is just an outer reflection of a more profound spiritual truth. Again, enforced equality, such as we have now, which tries to shoehorn everything into the same mould, will lead to disharmony and reaction. You cannot suppress the truth with ideology. Or you can try but there will be inevitable consequences if you do. But the demons win either way. They can corrupt our souls with their anti-truth/anti-God agenda or if there is a violent reaction to the lies they are making humanity believe, they can benefit from that too, from the negative emotions that ensue. They feed on hatred and anger. That is why it is important for any right-thinking person faced with all the insanity there is in the world to retain a certain distance from it and not get emotionally attached to opposition to it. It's an old trick of the devil to lie so hard that he entraps the virtuous into sin or imbalanced behaviour because of their outraged response to his lies. Don't allow yourself to be pushed into reaction. That's what the devil wants. If he can't get you on his side, he wants you to fight him because then he has drawn you into his orbit. So be wise to his tricks. Know his game of provocation and don't lower yourself to his level. Focus on the good and combat darkness by spreading light.

The lies will spread because we have cut ourselves off from objective truth which is God so there is nothing to anchor us to reality. Anything goes now. We can't stop that but what we can do is control our reaction to the lies. All we are responsible for is our self. We are living in today's world so that is where we are meant to be. That's fine. We just have to hold fast to the reality of God and then let what will be outwardly be. We will convince others more by quiet example than noisy confrontation. That doesn't mean you should be passive and let evil flourish. Fight it but don't fight it with its own weapons and don't allow the fight against it to stain your soul.

Most ordinary people reading the paragraphs above would think the writer deluded at best. Demons behind the scenes, manipulating our consciousness? That's crazy! But I think increasingly people will look at what's happening in the world and wonder how things can have come to this pass. Can humanity really have taken so many turns that completely defy common sense and are so against nature, let alone the idea of God as traditionally conceived? How have we allowed ourselves to be driven down this path, persuaded to abandon real goodness and truth in the name of a demonstrably false goodness and truth? I say demonstrably because practically every innovation we have allowed over the last 50 years, from on demand abortion to mass immigration to same sex marriage to the current push for transgender acceptance, goes against basic intuition. Obviously, all people should be treated with fairness and compassion but that is very different to normalising or even encouraging what is against the laws of God and creation. We are being programmed to think that what goes against nature is natural, and that must affect our connection to real truth. I mean it must affect us as in separate us from it and that is the demons' intention. It is our souls they are after but they do not want us to be dragged kicking and screaming into darkness. They want us to choose it as light.

Quite often today we are caught between two stools. We can see that injustice has been perpetrated on certain groups in the past. We rightly wish to remedy that. But appeals to compassion are exploited to bring about a situation in which the natural order of being is turned upside down and the baby of truth is thrown out with the bathwater of injustice. What we lack so much today is a balanced wisdom. We have discarded our spiritual inheritance completely instead of seeing that it needed a certain updating but was fundamentally sound. Jesus said he came to build on the Law and the Prophets. He did not come to replace them. These are words which we need to understand more than ever in the context of our present spiritual crisis.

The way forward is through love but not love as we currently understand it because we don't understand it. What we understand is an image of love, a theory about it with emotional overlays. Rarely do we feel love, not real love. We respond to life sentimentally which is what people do when they don't feel love deeply but want to or think they should. We know that love is the highest virtue and we try to live as if we loved or as how we think people who do love would live. But love comes from God. That is the only place it is situated, and only people who know God can know love as it is. Others act on a mixture of human emotions with some deeper feelings there too but without the real spiritual element.

Think of it like this. Love exists on all levels of reality; the divine, the spiritual, the human, the natural and even the material. It is what draws together. But it is only love in the proper sense on the spiritual and divine levels and there it is always one with understanding. These are the two sides of the one coin which is truth. The drive to equality comes from a false conception of love. It is love severed from understanding and misinterpreted as pertaining to the quantitative level. This is love despiritualised and materialised. In fact, love relates to quality. We do not love something for the fact that it is but for what it is. Its uniqueness. Everything God created is worthy of love unless it goes bad when it may still be loved for what it originally was and what it could be and for any good that remains in it but not for what it has made of itself. After all, badness doesn't exist as a basic reality. It is corrupted goodness. So, even the greatest sinner is essentially, as in originally, good. However, there are degrees of love and we love more that which has more of God in it, that which through inner growth manifests and is transparent to more of God. Even the saints who have become one with God are not equal because there is always more of God.

Don't You Want to Live in an Equal Society?

Most people believe, because they have been brought up to assume, that the ideal society is one in which everybody is equal. This seems an obvious truth if we respect fairness and justice and do not wish to perpetuate unfair privilege. The problem is it is entirely unnatural.

There is the idea that somehow a society in which everyone was equal would be a more spiritual society. But it would only be more spiritual in the way that materialistic people think of spirituality. That is as something that pertains and relates to human beings primarily as they are in this world. We say an equal society would be a fair society and that is good. But this is judging the purpose of human life as being fulfilled in a material world and disregarding the fact that there may be another, a higher, purpose behind life as we see and experience it in three dimensional, phenomenal terms. That life should be fair is the plaintive cry of the child but adults know it is just not fair. This doesn't mean we shouldn't try to make it more just, but it is a recognition that God has more important matters in his project for humanity than making things fair and equal here and now. There are deeper issues involved. To make something a priority which God has apparently not made a priority could be a mistake. A response to this might be that it is not God but man who has introduced inequality into society but that is an assumption. The degree of inequality has no doubt been influenced by men but not the basic fact of inequality which exists throughout nature.

Generally speaking, it seems to be the case that the more equal a society is nowadays, the more atheistic it becomes. Why should this be so? I would say it is because when you abolish hierarchy you also start to abolish the sense of higher and lower or even high and low. You reduce everything to a level playing field but that means there is no feeling of greater or lesser. The very idea becomes offensive. So God, as the archetypal greater, becomes less easy to accept. And this has ramifications beyond the loss of transcendence, ramifications which a society devoted to equality cannot fail to experience. Virtues that relate to hierarchy are lost, virtues such as nobility and honour, qualities such as glory and splendour, the very ideas of height and depth, all these are lost or, at least, greatly reduced in their meaning and significance. Cultural relativism becomes the norm because hierarchical distinctions are no longer tolerated. Everything's equal, after all. And then the sense of truth as an absolute begins to fade. It must because this again demands a hierarchical understanding of life and the appreciation that some things really are better than others because they correspond more to reality. Reality is not equal. It is there as a fact and you either accommodate to it to a greater or lesser degree or you don't. Right there, like it or not, is superiority and inferiority.

An equal society becomes one where mediocrity is the order of the day. It is one opposed to excellence of any sort and any condition, and where greatness is discouraged unless it is totally conformist which of course, by definition, it cannot be. If everyone is equal, this is the consequence. Such a society becomes one where people don't seek to transcend themselves in a vertical sense because the horizontal plane of being is given full priority. At some point the vertical plane, necessarily hierarchical, is just denied. It doesn't make any fundamental difference if you say that the equality you want is only one of opportunity. Once you introduce the idea of equality as a dominating principle of your society, it extends everywhere, and everywhere it beats all things down to its own level.

Now, clearly none of this means that a society should be ordered with rigid castes in which no one can rise, however exceptional they might be. Balance is required in all things, and hierarchical quality must be balanced with a sense of the inner oneness of humanity. But, and here's the point all egalitarians need to understand, if you make equality the cornerstone of your system as we increasingly do today when it has become the default assumption of what is good and right and to oppose it in any way is the sign of a bad person, then you are condemning your society to flatline mediocrity. You are going to bring the higher down to a level that is manageable by everyone. You are going to damage quality and ratify the medium and the average. Today we have reacted to a perceived excessive hierarchy of the past by rejecting hierarchy altogether as a fundamental principle. (It still exists but is disguised.) This has resulted in the impoverishment of culture and understanding. It goes hand in glove with materialism and the rejection of higher levels of truth and being. It leads to the reduction of human beings to their most basic elements.

It's also worth bearing in mind that those who are most insistent on equality are often those who feel themselves inferior in some way or another. Their motive is an unadmitted resentment and envy. From such impure beginnings, no true system can be built. We say it is desire for justice that drives this ideology. History, both distant and recent, proves that to be a naïve supposition in many cases.

Everyone wants to live in a just world. That is a worthy aspiration, though its realisation is probably a long way off. But to confuse this with a world of equality is a mistake. Equality is undue focus on one dimension of being but humans to be true to their humanity must know themselves to be multi-dimensional creatures, acknowledging both immanence and transcendence, inner and outer and so on. There is equality of intrinsic being but not of realised being. As was pointed out in the last chapter, even some of the saints stand closer to the throne of God than others though all have their fullness of the divine.

In ancient Egypt, which was probably the most spiritually ordered society there has ever been, there was no concept of equality. Men and women lived in a spiritual cosmos and served the gods in their allotted station. In ancient India the caste system served a similar purpose. From our modern perspective we might regard these as exploitative but in the context of their time they worked for everyone, high and low. Even if these societies may eventually have become corrupt they lasted for thousands of years and even now we can sense a kind of spiritual rightness about them. People of all classes lived in the light of truth because they understood that this world was the expression of a higher one and should be structured according to the divine pattern.

It might be said that Christianity changed this and made the world anew. It certainly did remake the world but it did not introduce equality and to claim so is to misapply the truths of spirit to the material realm. Making salvation available to all does not imply equality either before or after one is saved. In fact, there is now established a fundamental inequality between the saved and the not saved and the thing about equality is that, if it is real, it must be everywhere. You cannot have limited equality so if it is not everywhere, it is not anywhere.

The desire for equality is a desire of the fallen ego, the rebellious self that is motivated by envy and resentment. This goes back to Satan himself who desired to be equal to God and who corrupted our original parents by suggesting they too should aspire to be like the gods. To say this is not to condone exploitation of the lower by the higher but that is hierarchy gone wrong rather than the thing itself. You may as well reject love because of lust.

God created all souls as individual, all different, all unique. Equality means sameness, however you dress it up. That is what it must result in. The reduction of individuality to total conformity. What God wants his creation to grow into is the opposite of this. He wants us to become more individual though using that individuality to work with his creative purpose not in opposition to it and for itself. Even at the lowest levels of being there is no sameness. Every tree is different, every leaf is different, every blade of grass is different. God wants individuals and individuals are not equal. Equality is for machine-made things. It's no surprise that the desire for it arises in an age of materialism.

What Is the Great Modern Orthodoxy?

What is the one thing you cannot speak against without being regarded as wicked and immoral?

Is it not the idea of equality? This is the first principle of modern Western democracies and is applied to wider and wider fields. But what is its basis? Does it derive from the study of nature? One would assume it must but when you look for a possible origin, it is hard to find. For equality does not exist anywhere in nature and the belief in it has no reasonable foundation since people are very different. They are not the same so they are not equal. It's that simple. In fact, no two things in the created universe are the same. As we have just stated, the only things that are so are machine-made and these we describe colloquially but perceptively as having no soul. This leads one to think that perhaps the contemporary belief in equality is a consequence of the denial of soul which is the bedrock assumption of modernity. For modernity is based on the separation of Man from God. That is its defining characteristic.

No doubt the ideological belief in equality was also a reaction to the pronounced inequality that existed in the pre-modern age. But, like many reactions, it was an over-reaction and we went from one extreme to another. Or maybe from a perceived extreme to a real one. The further you get from truth, the more truth seems extreme. The idea of the oneness of humanity which gained currency from the eighteenth century onwards was also a factor. An inner oneness should not negate outer differences but the tendency of humanism has been in that direction as the rejection of spirit resulted in what belongs to that level of existence being brought down to and mis-expressed in the lower level as it can no longer be expressed in its proper sphere.

Equality taken to its logical conclusion means everyone, or even everything (for why stop at human beings?), is the same. There is no better and no worse. Everything is reduced to a uniform level which means that the idea of quality is undermined. You can either have quality or equality. You can't have both. We now live in an age in which quantity takes precedence over quality and it is therefore inevitably an age of general decline, intellectual, moral but most of all spiritual. This is the hidden side of democracy.

We need to restore balance but that will require such an upheaval in our current way of thinking that deeply entrenched beliefs which have grown up over 200 years will have to be thrown out. The idea of hierarchy will need to be re-established in some form, and people will have to accept that, though we all form part of the human family, we are not equal, certainly not as far as this world is concerned and probably not even the next. Perhaps if we replaced the word equality with justice we might make some progress. Equality means nothing. It describes nothing real. All human beings deserve respect but if you regard them all as equal you will destroy civilisation just as we are destroying it now. Besides, can you restrict equality just to people? Once you have started, where do you draw the line? These things have a tendency to move on to the next stage once they have established themselves, and even now there are many people who regard human beings and animals as equal. What this will mean in practice is that anything that separates humans from animals will be regarded as suspect. To make the higher and the lower equal here and now, you have only one recourse. You must bring down the higher.

Men are by no means equal on the earth plane but that is not a cause for dismissing anybody. With these words the Masters have summed up the situation. All human beings have intrinsic value in the eyes of God and all have the potential to become godlike. But that potential has been realised by only a few completely, the saints, and in some it has been totally lost, the demons. In between those two extremes there are as many shades as there are souls. By giving in to the illusion of equality we are actually destroying spirituality because we reduce it to something that no one has more of than anyone else. It becomes something that is within us all to begin with and does not need to be grown, developed and worked for, just realised. This both devalues the individual and flattens the transcendent. Goodness, truth, beauty and holiness are made meaningless. That is the end result of egalitarianism. Everything is reduced to nothing. Cosmos is returned to chaos, the only state of true equality.

*

I am a Christian and I am so for reasons both spiritual and intellectual. From the latter perspective you could say that Christ is the only thing that makes sense of the world. He is the only thing that answers every question you might have and many you may not have thought of. A Christian believes many things but one of the fundamental things he believes is that reality is made up of persons. Not things, not principles, not energies nor forces nor abstract ideas but persons, real, solid, concrete persons. God is the living God, personal, Christ is a person and we too are persons, created to manifest, grow and express our personhood and thereby enrich the universe by adding more glory to creation. All persons are equal, you might think but why would you think this? To be equal you must be the same and all persons are different. All persons are valid and justified and loved by God but the very fact of being a person creates inequality. Creation itself only comes about because of a disruption in the equality of nothingness.

A modern Christian is expected to believe in equality because Jesus preached that, didn't he? If he did it's not mentioned in the Gospels. I wonder if this misunderstanding has come about because of the Christian virtue of humility. Humility means that you do not think yourself better than others, and if you believe that then you must believe we are all equal. Such is the reasoning. But there is a big difference between not puffing yourself up with self-importance and thinking everyone is equal, If you think everyone is equal you must think you are the equal of the saints, even of Jesus himself. Is that what you think? Far from being a mark of humility, the belief in equality turns out to be more like a sign of pride.

If a Christian doesn't believe in equality, what then does he believe? First and foremost, Christianity is concerned with the spiritual not with this world. It is a supernatural religion, to do with the salvation of the soul which, as it stands, is in need of salvation. The default worldly situation is not that. Therefore, to be a disciple of Christ is to put supernatural reality at the centre of everything. Everything else, certainly everything in this world, is subordinate to that.

This is what I believe and what lies behind the basis of everything I have written here.

I believe in God the Father, Maker of Heaven and Earth. I believe that there was something approximating to the Fall when early humanity went against divine decree and that sin and death entered the world in the form we now know them. Clearly, sin must have potentially existed before as part of free will because what Adam and Eve did was sin but presumably this was the first actual sin. Similarly, death would have existed because I can't see Adam and Eve as existing in the Garden of Eden unchangingly forever but it would have been painless change without the suffering it acquired after the Fall. What prompted this Fall was the serpent tempting Eve with the possibility of equality with God. 'Ye shall become as gods.' Lucifer fell because he wanted to be equal to God and he tempted Eve with the same desire, awakening in her innocent heart the corrupting fires of envy and resentment. You don't have to take this story as literally true to see its profound symbolical veracity. Nor do you have to believe that Adam and Eve should never have eaten that apple. The Tree of Knowledge of Good and Evil was created by God so was good. The sin was not in eating the apple and thus awakening self-consciousness so much as in disobeying God and eating it before being ready to do so.

I believe that God sent Jesus to the world to redeem it from sin. This means that previously souls may have died and been reborn endlessly as many pagan religions believed with the only escape that discovered by the Buddha. There would have been time spent on the inner planes of being but there was no Heaven in the sense of union with God that is known in the beatific vision. Jesus, through his birth, death and resurrection, sanctified matter, removing the corruption of the Fall. He took on a material body and being free from any possibility of sin actually changed the structure of matter. Literally so for him, potentially so for anyone who followed him and allowed his life into theirs. This also meant that the individual soul, which is the point at which spirit and matter meet, could be sanctified and made whole, cured rather than killed.

I believe that Christ was the Son of God by which I mean he was not just an advanced spirit or higher being who had preceded us on the path. The attempt to cast him in this light may even be part of the ongoing demonic attempt to belittle Christianity. I cannot define exactly what Son of God means but I accept it on faith because it has the quality of the profoundest of truths. Attempts to reduce Christ to a special kind of prophet or enlightened soul are just wrong. He was and is something much more. I believe in all his miracles exactly as recounted in the Gospels and I absolutely believe in the Resurrection. With the Resurrection everything falls into place. It is the ground from which truth, goodness and beauty spring in the world. Without it there is only darkness and death.

I believe that Jesus was born through the Virgin Mary who was chosen for this mission because of her innate purity and goodness. I think that attempts to create a feminine spirituality in Gaia worship or something like that are atavistic and wrong. No one will get past the material and psychic worlds by following that path. The embodiment and pattern of feminine spirituality is the Virgin Mary, the Mother of God. A proper feminism, a truly spiritual feminism, would recognise that.

I believe in the saints and the Company of Heaven. I even believe I have encountered some of these beings who are the Masters I refer to here and there in these pages. I don't think that when such souls were in this world they were all Christian because I am sure that the spirit of Christ works through other religions, and that *the wind bloweth where it listeth* (John 3:8). But they now all serve under Christ. These saints seek to bring us up to their level but that requires us to open our hearts to truth, and truth exists on its own terms. We can never bend it to suit us.

I believe that Christ taught us that the major lesson on this Earth is self-sacrifice through love. All the attempts to attain higher consciousness that do not have this at their heart are doomed to failure because it is the key to Heaven. Christ taught this and demonstrated it in his life. He laid down the path and all we have to do is follow him.

There are many other things I believe about the spiritual world but these are the foundation stones of my approach to it.

An Attack on Cosmic Order

One of the areas in which the doctrine of equality has made greatest inroads is that of the relation between the sexes. It is now accepted almost everywhere and without question that feminism is about equality but there are two problems with this. The first is that it is not true, certainly not nowadays when many strands of feminism actively contest the masculine.

The second problem is that of equality itself. It is taken for granted that this is a reasonable objective, and that equality means everybody merits exactly the same thing. But if you look at both nature and the spiritual world there is no sign of equality in either of them. Indeed, as we have seen, if equality were a fundamental law of life there would never have been any manifested universe to begin with. Creation is based on inequality, the initial separation of heaven and earth being a rupture in oneness and the start of difference. Any kind of equality back then would have meant there could never have been any break in oneness. All would have remained eternally the same, dark, hidden, unexpressed. By the same token, difference is only possible with inequality and it is that which lies at the root of creation and cosmic order. The argument could still be put forward that we should grow into equality but that is hard to sustain in the face of a creative spirituality and a dynamic universe that does not subside into eternal rest. God creates to become more and to constantly exceed himself. This requires a certain imbalance which is the negation of equality.

Consequently, it should not be hard to understand that the contemporary assumption that oneness and equality are always good, even spiritual, things is a metaphysical mistake. This belief may not have arisen from the dark powers but is certainly encouraged and manipulated by them as part of their attempt to return creation to the state of chaos whence it arose. It underlies an attack on cosmic order, necessarily based on hierarchy, and is sustained by rebellion and resentment which are disguised and justified by the sentimental excuse of compassion. Not that compassion itself is sentimental but if used in a sentimental way which ignores or over-rules truth, it becomes destructive. This is disordered compassion or compassion that is not really compassion but simply dons its clothing in order to achieve an end desired by the sinfully motivated self. If the devil can quote scripture for his own ends, he can surely use virtue for his own purposes too. And he does.

As for men and women and a supposed equality between them, why not look to nature? We could, of course, look to scripture but that is rejected by most people nowadays when it conflicts with their agendas. However, we have an interesting example in nature with the phenomenon of handedness. Everyone is right- or left-handed. We do need both hands and so you could say that the hands are equal but one is the leader of the two and most of the time it is the right. There is a built-in imbalance and this appears to be one of the facts of life. Complete balance or symmetry does not occur. In the book *Towards the Mysteries* by Swami Omananda, the Masters have said, '**You should create without balance. Balance is not harmony. Balance is mechanisation of the mind.**' They were speaking of the arts but what they say applies to life in general too. Of course, it is because it applies to nature and life that it should apply to the arts, but the point is that balance is equality. Equality is not a desirable thing in terms of manifestation even if it might superficially appear to derive from pre-manifest oneness. But it does not exist in terms of created things and beings. Where do we see it? In the mineral kingdom, the plant kingdom, the animal kingdom, among humans? Nowhere is there a complete equality and nowhere could there be except in the darkness of primeval chaos. But light is never the same for there are always degrees of light. There are no degrees of darkness. If you think there sometimes are, that is only because that difference is created by light.

Going back to handedness and the undeniable fact that most people are right-handed, we should note that the association of the right side with the male and the left with the female is an ancient one that exists in many cultures. The two are complementary and do in a way balance each other but they are not the same and one is naturally the dominant one. This is just an example taken from nature and is not intended to prove anything. But I would say that it illustrates a general principle that should be obvious to the unprejudiced mind. It is not meant to be applied literally to the male/female complementarity but to show that nature is not interested in equality or perfect balance. Human beings are not hands but principles operate in a similar way throughout nature according to context. And note that if the left hand tries to dominate in a naturally right-handed person, the result will be a weakened state which is the situation we appear to be heading towards, our advanced technology (practically all created by males) tending to obscure that fact from us for the moment. By the way, I realise some people are ambidextrous but that is not the norm and this example is not intended to be pushed too far.

Many modern Christians who have lost touch with the transcendent reality of their religion and look at it largely in social terms think that Christ preached equality. The fact he didn't is part of the reason Judas Iscariot turned against him. Judas could not understand that Christ's kingdom was not of this world. He saw Jesus as a political figure, completely failing to grasp the message of spiritual redemption. This does not mean we should turn a blind eye to worldly injustices but it shows that equality was not a concern of Christ's, except insofar as he taught all people are potentially the children of God. Do you think that the man who said we would always have the poor with us thought that equality was attainable or even desirable?

No doubt if we lived in a world in which the strong did oppress the weak as a matter of course, in which the common humanity of all peoples was ignored or denied, and hierarchy abused (as, of course, it has been in the past), a reminder of the spiritual oneness of all human beings would be essential as long as that was fitted into an overall understanding of how human beings are also not equal in developed potential, expression, duties, responsibilities, spiritual unfoldment and so on. But the huge over-emphasis on equality today without a corresponding recognition of the hierarchical nature of cosmic order is separating us more and more from spiritual truth, and for that reason must be seen as instigated by the demons who are behind so many of the deviations of modernity as part of their attempt to reduce light to darkness.

I have mentioned the demonic employment of this doctrine of equality on several occasions. We need to understand how the powers that seek to lead humanity away from spiritual truth operate. Nowadays they rarely lie outright. We have evolved to a point at which we do have some rational grasp of basic moral ways of interacting with each other so that individuals and societies may function. Something that did not seem reasonably moral, even virtuous, would not work in a mainstream that no longer accepts might as right. Therefore, the trick is to take a truth and bend it so it becomes distorted. *Corruptio optimi pessima est.* In this case what is corrupted is the idea of the oneness of God and mankind. The demons have appropriated a spiritual truth and caused it to be misapplied to earthly existence so that real spiritual values are undermined.

The American Declaration of Independence has acquired the status of a religious document in some quarters. It is a remarkable work but it is not scripture. It famously declares that *We hold these truths to be self-evident, that all men are created equal.* I would say it is self-evident that is not the case but certain historians have put forward the idea that we have

33

misunderstood the meaning of the statement and that what Thomas Jefferson meant was that the American colonists had the same rights of self-determination as people of other nations. He was not referring to individual equality.

Be that as it may, the phrase was soon used to refer to individual equality and is now often brought forward to support the drive for ever greater egalitarianism. However, we should bear in mind that it has no antecedents in scripture or spiritual tradition. It is an eighteenth-century statement deriving from the likes of Thomas Hobbes and John Locke who were political thinkers. And while some may situate the origins of the egalitarian dogma in the biblical saying that we are all created in the image of God, this carries with it no implication of being created equal. It simply means we all have divine potential but that always needs to be actualised. Besides, after the Fall the image was damaged to a large degree so the fact that we are indeed all created in the image of God has no bearing on equality one way or the other.

Why would the demons wish to promote the idea of equality among human beings? What harm can it do? As it turns out, very great harm. Enthusiasts for this idea point to early human societies in which, they say, men and women lived in a state of oneness with nature and no rulers or ruled. Setting aside the obvious rejoinder that the suggestion is we return to a state of primitive barbarism with culture and civilisation at the most basic level, the fact is that it is just not true. In any society in which organisation of any kind exists there is some level of hierarchy. Given we see this even in the animal kingdom we should not be surprised.

This provides us with a clue as to what the demons' purpose might be. The more you return to the level of gross matter, the greater equality there is. Enforce equality on human beings and you take away their individuality. You reduce them to the level of an ant colony which is a mindless entity dedicated only to the survival of the colony. Equality destroys spirituality because spirituality demands freedom even if that freedom is simply to say 'Yes' to God when everyone else says 'No'. And equality, despite the slogan of the Enlightenment, destroys freedom. God created us individual and free. Equality makes us slaves.

What Is the Devil Most Seeking to Destroy?

First and foremost, this would be awareness of the spiritual but he doesn't want to stop there.

As an aside I should say that when I talk of the devil in these pages, I am speaking figuratively which is not to say that I do not believe in the existence of an entity corresponding to the devil in Christianity. I do, but I am not interested in this being as a person. That is God's business not mine. On the other hand, it is our business as human beings to be aware of the dark forces that seek to derail the spiritual progress of humanity and alienate us from God and our own souls, and I use the word devil as a shorthand to refer to these forces.

What the devil is most intent on attacking today after two centuries of gathering materialism is the natural order of being. If this were still intact, our spiritual loss would not be so grave and would be relatively easily recoverable. But once the natural order is undermined, anything goes. And this is increasingly the case. When we are separated from our own human nature and, what is worse, regard this separation as progress then we are indeed lost souls heading for destruction in one way or another.

The devil has sought to dismantle hierarchy which is the basis upon which the universe is built, the greater having its place in the scheme of things and the lesser having its own maybe not as important but still vital place. This hierarchical levelling includes the erosion of spiritual authority, the attack on the natural order with regard to male and female, old and young, intellectual and instinctual, the destruction of the sense of transcendence, the relativisation of values of higher and lower, more and less evolved and so on. All done in the name of equality which, as I hope to have made clear, is a false concept, existing only in the pre-creation state of non-manifestation, if it could even be said to exist there, and otherwise just an abstract theory.

Hierarchy can be abused, become inflexible and corrupted. In an imperfect world, things that are right in themselves can go wrong just as a normally healthy body can get sick. All levels have their rights and their duties, either of which can be ignored or forgotten, but a properly functioning hierarchy is still essential for a properly functioning civilisation with its roots in heaven and potential for growth in this world. Spiritual hierarchy sees all men as brothers but knows there are older and younger brothers who all live under one Father God and one Mother Nature. This union of spirit and matter produces souls, and souls all have individuality which is the opposite of equality.

The devil is well advanced along his path of the destruction of the natural order. This time he has acted not by overt force as in the two World Wars but by persuading a humanity softened up by the rejection of God that moral goodness requires recognising everyone as equal, whatever they are, because we are all human beings and that is primary. But this ignores the soul and it is the soul that gives quality and meaning to life. We who live in an age in which the transcendent is denied and the material seen as all there is are ripe for the picking. And picked we will be unless we start to wake up and no longer allow ourselves to be led astray by ideas that might sound reasonable on the surface but deny the deeper parts of our nature.

When God is denied then spiritual truth, which is truth itself, is lost. God doesn't force himself on us if we don't want him so he might be said to be at his weakest at this time. On the other hand, when the devil is denied he can be at his strongest because we take no precautions against him and easily fall into his traps which are just as effective against the clever as against the foolish. In fact, they are more effective against the clever who are never as clever as they think they are, particularly if they are not protected against error by some kind of genuine religious understanding which their cleverness makes them think they have outgrown. The foolish at least have instinct. The foolish would never think a man was a woman or that it's a sin to love your own kind above others. There is no one so stupid as a clever person.

We need to protect ourselves against the devil and this can be done on an individual or collective level. Collectively, it requires membership of a religion but religion has become moribund in most parts of the world and is far less spiritually sustaining than once it was. However, that can work to our advantage because now we are forced to build a personal relationship with God. The way can be harder and is more open to error if we are vain or unwise but the spiritual rewards can be greater too.

For those who do seek active engagement with the spiritual path one of the most important qualities to develop is discrimination. The ability to judge between good and evil, between truth and lies and to see the latter plainly, however cunningly it has been dressed up to look attractive. Today judgement is frowned upon because it separates and assigns a lower and higher place to things. It goes against equality. We emphasise Christ the merciful but he was judgemental too and if you don't believe that go back to your Bible. Christ was judgemental because he knew that we try to sneak into heaven carrying our sins with us but that simply won't work. Sins are like heavy weights that will drag us down and prevent us rising up out of material darkness. Christ was judgemental precisely because he was merciful. True mercy does not pander to darkness just so as not to have to be unpleasant. The devil knows how to use mercy to advance his agenda which is why mercy and compassion always have to be balanced with judgement and discrimination.

When Christ sent his disciples out to teach, he told them they would be like sheep among wolves. In our time that saying can apply to anyone who tries to walk the spiritual path. Christ went on to tell his followers that they needed to be as wise as snakes and as innocent as doves. Again, judgement and mercy. This is no less true for us today. The spiritual path is about wisdom just as much as it is about love and either one without the other is not just incomplete but false. Do not let the appeal to compassion blunt the sharp edge of wisdom.

There is a natural order of being that was laid down by God at the beginning of creation. The world works according to this pattern. It underlies the harmony of the universe. Observing this order helps us to transcend the limitations of the natural world because it reflects spiritual reality and points to higher truth. More is required than just this but it points us in the right direction. It prepares us for the journey. On the other hand, rejecting this natural order as we are being conditioned to do today will keep us locked in the material world because we do not even put our feet on the ladder that leads upwards. Heaven and Earth are very different but they have similarities too and if you would reach Heaven from Earth, you must observe the similarities. If you do not you will remain on the lower levels of being and you will find that even these levels lose what lustre they have as they become more separated from reality. Law and love arise from the same spiritual source and to deny one is to deny both. For they can only be known as they truly are when you go beyond them as they appear to be in this world and start to comprehend something of that which gives rise to them which is God.

Every rung on the ladder of life that leads from Man to God or Earth to Heaven is made of the same substance to which is added as you ascend something new in just the same way as a man contains something from the animal, vegetable and mineral kingdoms to which has been added the human soul. By denying the natural order the ladder collapses, leaving you cut off from God. The devil is trying to isolate us in the material world. This is why he seeks to overturn the order of nature which is the order of God.

The Elizabethan World Picture

Back in 1985 I was looking at some books my brother was throwing out. Among them was one that attracted my attention. It was written by an academic named E.M.W. Tillyard (1889–1962) and called *The Elizabethan World Picture*. I had recently read a couple of books by Frances Yates, a scholar who wrote several meticulously researched studies of Hermeticism during the Renaissance period, and this looked interesting. 'Could I take it?' I asked. It was an old school book and he didn't want it so I salvaged it from the pile of rejects.

The stimulus for this book was the attempt to get to grips with the metaphysical background to Shakespeare's plays and to Elizabethan literature in general. Tillyard realised that to understand the idea of political order during the period of the English Renaissance he had to see it as part of a much larger cosmic order. He found that this could be conceived in three ways which were as a chain, a set of correspondences and a dance. The notion of cosmic order ran through the whole of Elizabethan society and it was fundamentally religious in tone – as it would have to be since it was rooted not in the material world but in metaphysical reality. He saw that to imagine the Elizabethan age as a kind of precursor to secular humanism that was making the break from medieval religiosity, as was often the case at the time he was writing (1943), was wrong. It was much more the continuation and development of medieval thought and not really modern, as in anthropocentric, at all.

The basis of the Elizabethan understanding of the world was order. There was a divine order which was reflected externally in the Sun and the planets, and this order was expressed hierarchically. The proper working of this order and its proper recognition by Man resulted in harmony. Its neglect or abuse caused disharmony. It was like a musical instrument out of tune. And what principally caused disorder was sin.

The awareness of sin was everywhere in the sixteenth century as it had been in earlier centuries. The idea of sin and salvation was familiar to and acknowledged by all sections of the populace. And sin was spiritual in significance. Man's sin did not just affect him individually. It corrupted the world and set it out of kilter with its source. It severed the links in the chain that led down from God to Man.

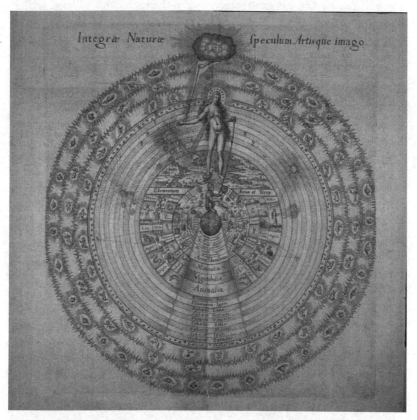

The Great Chain of Being from Robert Fludd's Utriusque Cosmi or Metaphysical History of the Two Worlds (1617). The hand of God reaches down through the stars to Nature and thence to the physical world.

The chain of being was the symbol that described both the connection of Heaven to Earth and its hierarchical nature. In Tillyard's words

'The metaphor served to express the unimaginable plenitude of God's creation, its unfaltering order, and its ultimate unity. The chain stretched from the foot of God's throne to the meanest of inanimate objects.' It bound the whole of creation together and each link took from above and gave to below which is not to say that the movement was always in one direction only. One of the significant aspects of this understanding of life was that even lower links in the chain brought something to the whole which was not otherwise present. Stones are near the bottom 'but they exceed the class above them in strength and durability'. So God is never wasteful and everything has its purpose.

Tillyard's book contains a full description of the various links in the chain as visualised by the Elizabethans, but for our purposes here it will be sufficient to list them briefly. All starts from God, naturally enough, and then proceeds down from him through the various hierarchies of angels until it reaches the stars 'which, though obeying God's changeless order are responsible for the vagaries of fortune in the realms below the moon'. Man, poised between heaven and earth, is the nodal point of this system and 'his double nature, though the source of internal conflict, has the unique function of binding together all creation, of bridging the greatest cosmic chasm, that between matter and spirit'. Below man there are the animal, vegetable and mineral kingdoms.

The chain describes the vertical aspect of the world but the horizontal is also catered for in this system. Here operate the correspondences which relate various things to others of a similar kind. However, the correspondences are not only horizontal, that is to say, connecting things on the same plane, for there are correspondences between celestial archetypes and earthly manifestations too. For example, the Trinity is reflected in man in understanding, will and memory, divine Intellect in the light of the sun and so forth. The correspondences in this regard demonstrate the wisdom of the famous Hermetic maxim. 'As above, so below.' The pattern of the heavens is repeated in things of the earth.

Finding connections is a game one can play endlessly and it can be illuminating too. However, I would refer the interested reader wanting to learn more to one of the many books on symbolism or even astrology which is largely based on a similar idea, the sense that all things in this world are reflections of higher ones and also connected to each other in various ways.

The last chapter in Tillyard's book is called The Cosmic Dance and it describes how traditionally creation had been thought of as an act of music. This idea is echoed in the creation myths of both Tolkien and C.S. Lewis which each start with music. God or the gods sing the universe into being. Tillyard quotes from 'A Song for St Cecilia's Day' by John Dryden (memorably set to music by Handel) which, though composed a little later in 1687, perfectly encapsulates the Elizabethan idea of creation.

> FROM harmony, from heavenly harmony,
> This universal frame began:
> When nature underneath a heap
> Of jarring atoms lay,
> And could not heave her head,
> The tuneful voice was heard from high,
> 'Arise, ye more than dead!'
> Then cold, and hot, and moist, and dry,
> In order to their stations leap,
> And Music's power obey.
> From harmony, from heavenly harmony,
> This universal frame began:
> From harmony to harmony
> Through all the compass of the notes it ran,
> The diapason closing full in Man.

But it is not just creation that is understood musically. The dance goes on everywhere at all times, the movement of the planets being a notable instance of it. The sea dances to the music of the moon. Time itself is said to be a kind of dance. Movement is musical. Life is musical. And it is no accident that courtship was thought to revolve around dancing. That idea survives today, even if in a much degraded form. You could probably judge the state of a society's civilisation by the sort of dances it favours. Which is bad luck for us.

These three things, the great chain of being, universal correspondences and the dance of life were at the heart of the Elizabethan conception of the universe. This was seen as existing both horizontally and vertically with all its component parts related to each other, all having a place in the scheme of things to which they should keep if the whole was to continue in harmonious fashion. This did not rule out growth and development, but that should be in line with the naturally unfolding patterns of life and not be in an arbitrary, chaotic, forced or wilful way which would surely introduce disorder and destroy harmony.

I am not saying that the image of the world as understood by the Elizabethans is literally true but, as a symbolic representation of how the universe is organised, it is considerably more accurate than anything we have today. We now live in a world that has abandoned any higher sense of how the universe works and has consequently introduced the level of disorder that all traditional teaching warned about if the laws of life were disregarded and human egotism allowed full sway. We have disrupted universal order and one of the principal ways we have done so is through the levelling of hierarchy. For the Elizabethans this would have seemed a reckless act of destruction that extended far beyond the political sphere into the spiritual. It would have been regarded as tantamount to chopping down the ladder of life that joined human beings to God for the attempt to establish equality divorces Earth from Heaven by removing the links in the chain that connect them.

The Descent of Man and the Prophecy of Hermes

This is a time of inverted values when good and evil become blurred and lose their definition. We call this progress because we have lost connection to spirit and transcendent reality but it more resembles the contraction of being to the plane of matter which, without spirit, tends towards chaos as in unqualified formlessness. It can never actually reach that state because spirit exists and holds things together whether we believe in it or not but it can approach it and the less we do acknowledge transcendence, the closer we will come to it.

The descent from spirit to matter is recognised in traditional teachings on the four ages which descend from Gold to Silver to Bronze to Iron. The Golden Age is fully open to spirit. This was the world now only known to us in myth when gods walked the Earth and civilisation and culture were based on reconstructing the pattern of the heavens. Authority was with sacred leaders who were in touch with the higher worlds and transmitted the sense of those worlds to the populace who themselves instinctively responded to the reality of spirit.

The law of entropy applies to cycles of human existence as it does to everything in the material world. As time passed, consciousness became more constricted and the material world more present. Leadership passed to the second caste, a warrior aristocracy of kings and nobles. There was still a strong sense of the spiritual but the affairs of this world began to assume a greater prominence. This, by the way, only applies to more advanced sections of humanity who were able to form coherent civilisations. Primitive peoples existed in the typical state of closeness to the earth, generally speaking unable to separate themselves from nature to any significant extent.

Here we should point out that the whole of historical time is regarded as part of a greater Iron Age when matter is the main focus of conscious awareness and spirit has fallen from its rightful pole position. But there are cycles within cycles, patterns are repeated on higher and lower levels, and the descent from Gold to Iron is repeated even within the Iron Age itself as it is within all authentic human civilisations. The ages as I describe them here should be understood in that context.

The descent to the third phase comes when aristocracies degenerate, losing touch with their core virtues such as honour, chivalry, loyalty and responsibility for those over whom they stand. Power now shifts to money and those who trade, the merchant or, in modern terms, the banker and the industrialist. The economy is of central concern and higher values begin to be lost and replaced by utilitarian ones appropriate to the material plane on which attention is now concentrated, thrift, industriousness and practicality. Equivalent vices come into play too. But then there comes a further descent and power begins to shift to what was traditionally regarded as the lowest caste, what we today call the people or the masses. Simply by virtue of their greater numbers they start to become of significance. We have entered the age of quantity in which matter assumes the prerogatives of spirit with the consequent inevitable loss of all higher values relating to truth, goodness and beauty considered as spiritual realities. This is clearly the age we are now in though it must be recognised that there is always overlap between ages. We might regard this new phase as starting around the time of the French Revolution, given a large boost with the Russian Revolution and now spreading throughout the West. Even if the masses do not yet have actual political power, as the merchant class still holds onto that in most places, they can influence it enormously, and they undoubtedly have cultural power due to their increased financial power and also the fact that materialism is the default belief system even among many religious people who effectively relegate their religion to a subset of an overall materialistic world view. The current dogma of egalitarianism is a tell-tale sign of the descent of power to the mass population.

We can see the decline of spiritual influence in every area of human life as would naturally be the case since it is a universal phenomenon that primarily affects consciousness though the psychological and physical environments also coarsen. Art, which began as sacred then became high and is now more or less just popular, is an obvious example but you can see the descent everywhere. Nothing is exempt, including, and in some ways especially, religion.

I don't reject Darwin's theory of evolution as a partial explanation of how animal forms developed but it is very one-sided. Unlike the two other apostles of modernism with whom he is sometimes bracketed, namely Marx and Freud, he was clearly a serious scientist engaged in serious work which could have brought about, if regarded as applying only to certain aspects of the creative/evolutionary process, a real advance in understanding. But unfortunately, it was taken as a complete description of how life developed and grew. It has become the creation myth of the materialist and the harm it has done is seldom recognised. For what it did was to reduce Man to a creature that ascended from the mud instead of descending from the stars, and it is used as a justification for much of the spiritual degradation we see today. If we are solely material, only material values matter. We are all equal, all equally nothing. If we come from the mud then mud is basically what we all are *au fond*.

The modern attempt to establish equality is part of the general spiritual decline. It might seem well-intentioned but good intentions do not justify error. Greater equality is not a Christian aspiration. God loves all his children and they all have their rightful place on the ladder of life but the ladder has many rungs as it must if we are to ascend. In terms of fulfilling the purposes of creation, movement into the authentic spiritual demands increased differentiation with each soul needing to realise the fullness of its individuality in order to evolve into a higher state of being. Equality means sameness and can only be truly present if all spiritual order and structure break down. For if there is form of any kind there must be inequality. The movement towards greater equality might appear to be driven by a desire to atone for injustices of the past, but the actual effect is to remove higher values and truths. It does not elevate but flattens.

This does not imply society should strive towards greater inequality. That is to think in political terms and we have to learn to approach social questions from the metaphysical perspective, seeing life in its wholeness rather than just the material part. A proper spiritual focus will guide us in how our worldly societies should be constructed and what they exist to achieve. We have to understand the purpose of mortal life and that it is not sufficient unto itself. This means we don't attempt to do things in this world without knowing something of the next. Matter should conform itself to spirit. The drive towards egalitarianism is doing the opposite, and this applies to such modern preoccupations as racism and sexism, concerns that barely registered in traditional societies because they had not separated themselves from their natural instincts.

Not being racist used to mean white people not being nasty to black people, treating them fairly and honestly. But then it changed and meant not acknowledging there was any reality to the concept of race at all and that all groups were equal in every respect with no distinguishing characteristics apart from superficial ones like skin colour.

Not being a sexist used to mean not behaving badly towards women, treating them with proper respect. Then it meant not acknowledging there was any difference between men and women at all and that they were both fundamentally the same, except physically of course, and now even the physical differences are being challenged .

The question is, does any of this matter? Is it just the inevitable over-reaction as human beings move towards creating a more equitable society with things eventually sorting themselves out? Or is it a real problem as natural hierarchies are disrupted with the result a collapse of civilised values and a divided world. Is it a recipe for increased harmony and justice or will it lead to a descent into chaos and antagonism? There is an answer to these questions and it is provided by an ancient text. Our current world mirrors the state of affairs predicted in the Prophecy of Hermes which concerned what would befall ancient Egypt but which can also be seen to apply to us today since the downfall of civilisations generally follows a similar pattern. The text in the form that has come down to us was written in Greek long after the demise of ancient Egypt, perhaps between 100 and 300 AD, so may well be a case of being wise after the event, but that doesn't affect its prophetic relevance for the present time.

Since it is fitting that wise men should have knowledge of all events before they come to pass, you must not be left in ignorance of this: there will come a time when it will be seen that in vain have the Egyptians honoured the deity with heartfelt piety and assiduous service; and all our holy worship will be found bootless and ineffectual. For the gods will return from earth to heaven.

Egypt will be forsaken, and the land which was once the home of religion will be left desolate, bereft of the presence of its deities.

This land and region will be filled with foreigners; and Egypt will be occupied by Scythians or Indians or by some such race from the barbarian countries thereabout....

Do you weep at this, Asclepius? There is worse to come; Egypt herself will have yet more to suffer; she will fall into a far more piteous plight, and will be infected with yet more, grievous plagues; and this land, which once was holy, a land which loved the gods, and wherein alone, in reward for her devotion, the gods deigned to sojourn upon earth, a land which was the teacher of mankind in holiness and piety, this land will go beyond all in cruel deeds. The dead will far outnumber the living; and the survivors will be known for Egyptians by their tongue alone, but in their actions they will seem to be men of another race.

O Egypt, Egypt, of thy religion nothing will remain but an empty tale, which thine own children in time to come will not believe; nothing will be left but graven words, and only the stones will tell of thy piety. And in that day men will be weary of life, and they will cease to think the universe worthy of reverent wonder and of worship. And so religion, the greatest of all blessings, for there is nothing, nor has been, nor ever shall be, that can be deemed a greater boon, will be threatened with destruction; men will think it a burden, and will come to scorn it. They will no longer love this world around us, this incomparable work of God, this glorious structure which he has built....

Darkness will be preferred to light, and death will be thought more profitable than life; no one will raise his eyes to heaven; the pious will be deemed insane, and the impious wise; the madman will be thought a brave man, and the wicked will be esteemed as good. As to the soul, and the belief that it is immortal by nature, or may hope to attain to immortality, as I have taught you, all this they will mock at, and will even persuade themselves that it is false...

And so the gods will depart from mankind, a grievous thing! and only evil angels will remain, who will mingle with men, and drive the poor wretches by main force into all manner of reckless crime, into wars, and robberies, and frauds, and all things hostile to the nature of the soul...

After this manner will old age come upon the world. Religion will be no more; all things will be disordered and awry; all good will disappear.

But when all this has befallen, Asclepius, then the Master and Father, God, the first before all, the maker of that god who first

came into being, will look on that which has come to pass, and will stay the disorder by the counterworking of his will, which is the good. He will call back to the right path those who have gone astray; he will cleanse the world from evil, now washing it away with water-floods, now burning it out with fiercest fire, or again expelling it by war and pestilence. And thus he will bring back his world to its former aspect, so that the Kosmos will once more be deemed worthy of worship and wondering reverence, and God, the maker and restorer of the mighty fabric, will be adored by the men of that day with unceasing hymns of praise and blessing.
(From the Book of Asclepius, translated by Walter Scott)

On the face of it this is depressing stuff but we need to keep in mind the conclusion of this prophecy. It is echoed in Indian religion where Krishna restores the good after a period of universal collapse. We may be living in times of spiritual darkness now but the longer view might see this as part of a larger pattern when all incipient evil is brought out so that it may be cleansed away and the ground prepared for spiritual rebirth. In the greater scheme of things this may be no more than a tilling of the soil and an uprooting of weeds that have grown up over the previous periods of development. In the end the only lasting reality is that of God.

Against Inequality

The premise of this book is that the concept of equality belongs to the domain of measurement but has mistakenly been applied to the human world or world of living things which are worlds of quality. Equality is a quantitative idea and so it is not surprising that it should be adopted in this way during an age of materialism, a time when even religion is regarded not so much as concerned with higher worlds and immortal destiny as being a good neighbour in the context of this world. Jesus said love your neighbour as yourself. What, to a spiritually oriented person, is the most important thing? It is salvation, spiritual realisation, whatever you wish to call it. Therefore, loving your neighbour as yourself means before anything else giving him the chance to grow spiritually.

But if equality is a false doctrine, and especially so when, as today, it is used to chop down higher understanding, that does not mean we should promote, encourage or enforce inequality. The truth of the matter is that to regard human beings in terms of equality *or* inequality is to look at them in the wrong way. Everything is what it is, unique and individual. People are not equal but nor are they unequal as we usually understand those terms. That doesn't mean that there are not higher and lower or more evolved, as in having unfolded more of the divine nature, and less evolved. There surely are and the higher is superior to the lower but it is not, if I can put it this way, better. Is a lion superior to a snail? In one way, it certainly is but it is not a better snail and a snail is part of God's creation. Is an archangel superior to a run of the mill type person who will never amount to much? Obviously he is but God loves them both, and they both have a divine destiny. To repeat the Masters' words which are the seed from which this book has grown, **men are by no means equal on the earth plane but that is not a cause for dismissing anybody**.

They said something else that is relevant to the present discussion. This was on the subject of pride and humility, a favourite topic of theirs as far as I was concerned. They said that if you are to help somebody, you must make them feel an equal. No one can accept anything if he feels he is being spoken down to. The greatest souls treat others with complete respect and this is not because of self-conscious spiritual behaviour but because they really see the divine image in a person. The fact that we all have the divine image within us does make us, in a certain sense, equal even if equality is not the proper way to frame this. It's more accurate to say that God is in everyone and that makes everyone worthy of respect. A small error in your aim can make you completely miss the target.

Once we abandoned a religious mindset we had to invent a morality based on man conceived as a material being with no spiritual background or destiny. Spiritually speaking and in terms of evolving consciousness, the idea of equality has no meaning. It only acquires a potential relevance when men and women are regarded as existing solely in this world and as being no more than they appear to be here. Then you must find a way in which they can relate to each other and get on with each other. You can either have a world in which everything is reduced to power or you can have a world in which human beings are seen as equal with the same rights. In practice, you can have a mixture of the two in which power still dominates behind the scenes but equality is the basis of public morality. This is more or less what we have now.

The idea of equality is a red herring that only arises because we have a false image of what a human being is. That is why framing the discourse in terms of inequality would also be wrong. Human beings are neither equal nor unequal because they are spiritual. The spiritual world is not one of measurement so it is not one of equality. It is interesting to note that the Sanskrit word *maya* often translated as illusion actually refers to the idea of measuring, with *ma* meaning to measure and *ya* meaning that. So *maya*, which is the principle of form, properly means that which measures or that which can be measured. The spiritual is not measurable and therefore the notion of equality is not applicable there. But so is the notion of inequality. There are greater and lesser manifestations of divine being and that is all.

Traditional metaphysics understood the universe to be constructed hierarchically. The great chain of being stretched from the throne of God down into the depths of matter as we saw depicted in the Elizabethan world picture. Likewise, human beings are organised in a hierarchical manner with rulers and ruled, wise and foolish, strong and weak and so on with many gradations between top and bottom. The caste system of India and the class system elsewhere both reflected this basic understanding. But something changed with Christianity. What changed was not that hierarchy was replaced by equality though some understood the matter in this way. What changed was that the lower was now accorded its proper value. It was still the lower but it too was part of God. In the Masters' words: **Beauty is everywhere. It varies in degree according to its closeness to God but there is God in everything and that means beauty**.

So, there is still greater beauty and lesser beauty, greater wisdom and lesser wisdom, more evolved and less evolved human beings, but everything is imbued with the presence of God. Christ brought a new understanding of the meaning and responsibilities of hierarchy. The higher would now serve the lower and yet, for one must not misunderstand this, this would only work if the lower recognised the higher as higher. It is not that roles are reversed but Christ added to a spirituality of knowledge a spirituality of love. That is what this new view of hierarchy means. It does not mean equality. Christ treated his disciples as equals but they certainly did not regard themselves in that light. Christ washed the feet of his disciples but they still followed him as Christ. The hierarchy remains but it is viewed differently. To abolish it would mean that spirit is brought down to the level of matter and the greater to the lesser. The Christian view is not that the ladder that leads to God is destroyed but that those on the higher rungs reach down with love to those below.

I have called this book By No Means Equal which is a quotation from the Masters. But the full quotation reads '**men are by no means equal on the earth plane**'. This means men (and women, of course) are not equal in this world and never will be. But can one perhaps infer from this that there is equality in higher worlds, in heaven? No, for there is no equality anywhere, not even in heaven. In heaven all souls are one in Christ. They are all filled completely with God but each individual soul's capacity for being filled with God, the amount of God each can be filled with, differs. A soul can certainly increase its capacity as heaven is not a place of static, unchanging oneness. The ascended soul can always travel more deeply into the heart of God and become aware of ever greater dimensions of divine being. You can grow in heaven but it is not a place in which all are equal. If it were there would be no room for further expansion and that would be a kind of limitation. Heaven would have a roof instead of being open to the infinite.

Body, Soul and Spirit

If we are equal where does this equality lie? Obviously, it doesn't lie in the body. This person has more beauty, that person has more strength, this person has better eyesight, that person has better general health. Nor does it lie in the mind. This person is more intelligent, that person is musical, this person is artistic, that person is good at maths, this person is dyslexic, that person is autistic and so on. You might say that compared to a chimpanzee all humans are more or less equal but that doesn't make them equal in terms of what they are any more than a human and a chimpanzee being more or less equal compared to a rock makes them equal in any real sense.

According to the spiritual perspective a human being is threefold, being comprised of spirit, soul and body. You can break this down further into the physical body, the emotional nature and the mind as our material self, the soul as our spiritual self or individuality and spirit which is our divine being and connection to God. Spirit is where we are one with God. It is the spark from the divine fire. Few of us are conscious on that level. The goal is to become so.

We have already pointed out that equality cannot be found in the material self. Our bodies, emotions and mental faculties may all be similar and founded on the same principles but they are not the same. Might that mean equality can be found in the spiritual world? Are our souls equal? If they are all individual, wouldn't that give them a rough kind of equality?

A rough kind of equality is meaningless. Equality means equality. No one would deny that human beings share a common humanity but that is quite a different matter to equality. We all have physical bodies, two arms, two legs, a brain and a heart but so do monkeys and even if we restrict ourselves to humans, the quality of the bodies are hugely different. But does the fact that we are all individuals still give us a general equality? Surely if it did it would mean that no individual could be better, superior or more evolved, however you want to put it, than another.

But this is not the case. In just the same way as bodies can be stronger or weaker so souls can be more developed or less so in the sense that they are more attuned to the spiritual world and more able to manifest and express its qualities or else not fully awake to higher forms of consciousness. Individual souls are not created fully grown. They have to develop themselves through their efforts and experiences in the material and spiritual worlds. Some souls may have been created earlier; some souls may have taken opportunities that others have missed. Not all human souls may come from the same spiritual source.

The fact is there is even less equality in the spiritual world than there is in the material. Inequality is actually more pronounced on the level of the soul than it is on the levels of the body and the mind. That this is not always apparent in the material world is because the spiritual is not fully expressed or expressible here. This is a three-dimensional plane of being and spiritual consciousness includes further dimensions of awareness that are not known, or very imperfectly known, in this vibratory spectrum. That's why many sensitive souls feel themselves to be trapped in a limited world, mind and body constricted as though they had been spiritually crippled. As indeed they have been though that is a necessity if they are to learn their lessons which require focus on the material world and the sense of separation that goes with that.

I know from my experience with the Masters, who are spiritual beings operating from the spiritual world, how wide the inequalities can be. The thought that I was in any way equal to them is frankly laughable. Not that they ever made me feel unequal or inferior but I clearly was. This is not just a question of age, although that is a factor especially if you widen the definition of age to include spiritual age. But it was principally to do with consciousness. They had mastered full receptivity and response to the higher dimensions of the spiritual world and were able to express that within the context of their individualities. It's a question of development and expansion into higher levels of being. Think of this in terms of light. The Masters are able to look into the sun without being blinded.

This may be an extreme example but the disparities exist throughout the human kingdom which runs the gamut from those souls not much more advanced than the beasts right up to saints and sages. I don't say from sinners to saints because some sinners can be highly developed in many ways even if spiritually, they are not. But repentance and reorientation of the heart can put that right more quickly than it could with the less evolved who would still have to develop their human nature, personal, intellectual and spiritual, before becoming ready to step into full divine consciousness.

Some people, following St Paul in Galatians 3:28 where he writes that 'There is neither Jew nor Greek, slave nor free, male nor female for you are all one in Christ Jesus', would contend that, while inequalities may exist in worldly terms, in the spiritual world we are all equal. One isolated quotation is hardly conclusive but even if this did mean there was equality in Christ it also means there is inequality apart from Christ so any equality would depend on the full acceptance of Christ to be effective and would not exist outside that context. But actually that is beside the point anyway because to be one in Christ does not mean to be equal. It means to be one. If I become a Christian, am I then Francis of Assisi's equal? St Paul's? Christ's? Obviously not. What St Paul meant was that you will have a spiritual unity in which outer differences drop away in terms of them being significant barriers to unity so all are members of the same brotherhood if they accept Christ, but their individual differences will remain. These are just not obstacles to the sense of oneness which has superseded them as the dominant factor of consciousness.

There is no equality on the material level and no equality on the spiritual level which is the level of the soul. But what about the level of spirit, the level of divine being? You might speculate that at this level of complete nakedness where we are stripped even of our self, there is an equality before God. This is where we are effectively nothing. It is the core of our being, before manifested and expressed differences have arisen. This is where the image of God is planted in us and every human soul has that image. However, this equality at the very root of our existence must always go with the inequalities at the created levels. A human being is not spirit alone. He is spirit, soul (self) and body (outer expression), a three in one, and the equality at the level of spirit never actually exists in terms of the expressed self though it underlies that expression and is the cause of the oneness that exists between all souls in heaven where they are one in God but also fully themselves. As long as anything is something, which by definition it must be, there can be no equality.

Part II

Secular Spirituality

One of the difficulties of living in the present day is that not only is it a time of materialism and atheism but that when individuals do turn to the spiritual they often take large chunks of the materialistic, atheistic culture in which they grew up with them. They retain the inbuilt assumptions of the secular world even when supposedly renouncing that world. Nowadays this is usually in the form of a more or less leftist ideology which most people don't realise derives from a rejection of God and religion, and the attempt to replace spiritual reality with a secularised vision of life with the earthly human being at its centre. As a result, their version of spirituality is a post-Enlightenment/post-French Revolution version, both of which either dismissed the spiritual or brought it down to the rational. Such people are left with a form of spirituality which is focused on humanity and human potential rather than God and that gives them a kind of cognitive dissonance. The fact is we always need to see the spiritual in its own terms and from its own perspective not through our worldly human eyes. But this is just what many people now do. They see the spiritual as something that should operate to benefit the human person as that person is here and now in its fallen state.

This means you can now have spirituality without repentance which is a sorry distortion of the truth. Healing may be an aspect of the spiritual path but spirituality is not therapy and when the two become confused you have a focus on human psychology and the 'me', even if you dress that up as the 'me' seeking to encompass what is beyond itself.

I have heard people claim that spiritual feelings are natural human feelings and that you can pursue spiritual values and believe in transcendence, love, peace, wisdom etc. without worrying about God or Christ or the afterlife or anything religious. They are mistaken. Your feelings are not truth. They might be based on truth but they might be based on a lot of other things too, and they are still just your personal feelings. You must go beyond them to their real source. And their real source, if they are authentic and not just wishy-washy indulgences, is God. You cannot separate the unripe fruit from the tree or you can but if you do the fruit will quickly start to decompose. That is the problem. Unless you root your spiritual feelings in their source they will remain undeveloped and then decay, becoming imitations of reality that you feel you feel but don't know deep down.

Modern forms of spirituality are often just psychological therapies and ignore the spiritual fundamentals of repentance and belief in God. You are not a child of God now simply by believing yourself to be so. The bridge to that state, if it is to be known and lived correctly, remains narrow, the sacrifice demanded remains extreme for it is that of your worldly self. That self as it is cannot be spiritualised which is a common error made by those whose idea of spirituality is their feelings. It must be given to God. Not as a theory but in reality, and for this to be real demands full acceptance of God as a real being not just some vague, amorphous abstraction that you keep at a safe distance.

You might think you can have spirituality without God but that is a trick of the devil. The only valid approach that has ever tried that is the Buddhist one which is why Buddhism is popular among the spiritually deracinated these days. But two things need to be understood. Firstly, Buddhism was traditionally always a monastic religion, and I emphasise both words. Buddhism may not have been theistic but it still demanded an intensely religious approach not a secular one. And two, for all the later attempts to compensate for this, Buddhism is essentially a creation-rejecting spirituality which denies the goodness of the self. But God had a purpose in creation. His aim was not to return to the unformed state but to bring the beauty of matter into harmony with the truth of spirit and make something new.

But anyway, contemporary secular spirituality often owes more to Jung than the Buddha, and while Jung is praised for bringing the psychological up to the spiritual you could just as well say he did the opposite and brought the spiritual down to the psychological level thereby secularising it and robbing it of its spiritual integrity and power.

Here then is the problem. How can we lead an authentic spiritual life in the modern world without having that undermined by the materialistic ideology that is everywhere? How can we cleanse our minds, purging them of every aspect of secular materialism? This is the task that lies before us at the present time because materialism can be like a worm in the apple of the mind and contaminate the whole thing unless it is removed completely. Unfortunately, all of us are corrupted by it to some degree as it is the intellectual environment in which we have lived, moved and had our being for our entire earthly existence. It's the basic assumption to everything, how we are educated, our culture, high and low, and it drives our dreams and ambitions. It's all pervasive. Even many people who believe they believe in God are materialists with their religious beliefs sitting in an overall context of present-day secular materialistic assumptions such as democracy, humanism, feminism and so on.

I mention feminism. Our current world is sometimes described as increasingly feminised and this doesn't just refer to the rise and spread of feminism over the last hundred or so years. It also describes the attitudes that prevail in contemporary society as a whole, over and above the roles of men and women, and it will inevitably lead to spiritual loss. Here's why.

A feminised society tends to promote safety and security over other considerations. It wants what is most agreeable to most people without excessive challenge or discomfort. Women generally observe the status quo. It is men who take risks and break boundaries so a feminised society will value security and conformity above all. As a result, it will start to regress to a kind of childhood. These characteristics, excellent and necessary in a mother, are an ideal balancing corrective to the more masculine drive that seeks out truth and creates a civilisation. They can temper that drive and control its excesses. However, if they dominate as they are beginning to do now they infantilise and weaken and lead to a reversal of cultural achievement.

The childlike condition that results might be regarded as spiritual in that it bears a slight resemblance to pre-agricultural societies that supposedly lived in harmony with the natural world in a state of peace and communal equality. I have to stress supposedly since more recent, less ideologically driven research has shown that to be mostly a fantasy. But even assuming it were true, societies of this kind remained just as they were for thousands of years. They never advanced until disturbed, and their spirituality was largely just an awareness of the supernatural. They had not begun to grow into a real knowledge of God, and the purpose of life in this world is to transform human souls from a state of passive participation in life into beings of creative love and power. In short, to make gods. This requires constantly aspiring upwards, reaching beyond the safe and what is acceptable and attainable by everybody in the society. It demands that we leave spiritual childhood behind and become spiritual adults which means abandoning the lowlands and climbing mountains. Like it or not, and many religious people won't in an egalitarian age, a truly spiritual attitude needs the pioneering spirit. A feminised society is one whose members stay in the nest and will never fly.

It can easily be observed that both materialism and feminism arise at the end of a civilisation's lifetime. They appear to be signs of cultural fatigue and decay and arise from a loss of spiritual purpose, coming about when the creative impulse that forms a civilisation has worn out and it is living off its past achievements.

Duality is the basis of the manifested universe. It is the interplay between two opposing forces that brings about creation and drives evolution. It could be said that Man only begins to know himself because of Woman and vice versa. Therefore, to point to feminism as a sign of cultural collapse is not to criticise woman any more than to condemn materialism is to condemn matter. Just as the devil doesn't lie outright so much as deform the truth, the problem here is that womanhood and the material have been taken out of place and made to usurp the role of that which they are intended to complement in the context of duality. They have been made to become, or try to become, what they are not which results in disorder and spiritual chaos. If you don't recognise this in our modern world it's because you don't understand spiritual order. The devil is not very imaginative. He always makes the same offer. Give me your soul and I will give you money and/or power. He's played his usual game with feminism and materialism, and many people have made the exchange.

How do we grow out of this? By starting to take the teachings of Christ seriously. These are not adjuncts to the modern beliefs of the world and the secular ideologies of materialism, as they often seem to be perceived nowadays. They completely replace these ideologies, showing them to be shallow impostures deriving from a false idea of the soul. Feminism is an offshoot of secular materialism but when the feminine is rededicated to the spiritual it is transformed and becomes a sacred vessel for the divine as with Mary. Similarly with matter. Just as with the soul itself, these things only find their true fulfilment when they give themselves over to God through Christ. Then they become the holy things they always potentially are. At the moment they have been deformed by trying to be something they are not.

God, Man and Woman

It has been observed that women in Christian parts of the world used to be more religious than men but are now less so. No doubt you could widen this to include other religions but Christian apostasy is further down the road than that of other religions. The premise is that the feminine psyche is more conformist so will adapt itself to the prevailing culture, but it is also more concerned with being, and being perceived as, good. If what society deems good really is good that is an excellent thing but when, as now, society has been corrupted by materialism, atheism and their cultural consequence which is leftism, it is disastrous.

One can see why so many women adopt feminism even though that means undermining their true being. It appears to promise them so much and claims to redress error and set right injustices of the past. It comes in a shiny package and appeals both to egotism and resentment, carefully rebranding these as noble sentiments – an old trick of you know who. But everything it offers is on the material plane and even there its gifts are poisoned. Spiritually, it is entirely regressive which is why when it moves into spiritual matters it is always on the old pagan, Gaia worship level which is something humanity should have long outgrown even if Nature and the Feminine have been undervalued in the West since at least the time of the Reformation. But that is a different matter. You don't correct error by making more error. The fact is that the story in Genesis concerning Adam and Eve represents a profound truth about the created order and points to the path of fulfilment and truth for both sexes. In the Bible God created Woman as a companion and helper for Man but this does not make him superior as headship in Biblical terms is not over her but in the context of a loving union. Nor should it be the cause of any resentment. It is just a simple fact that corresponds to the nature of each sex's being and to which both sexes should strive to make themselves worthy. It's a partnership with each partner having different roles and loving, honouring and fulfilling the other. To rail against it is an act of rebellion, one that comes from pride and the ego, and to upset this order puts Woman at odds with the truth of her own nature and thereby creates disorder. At the same time, to abuse it on the masculine level, which no one can deny has happened throughout history, is also completely wrong. The partnership is based on love and mutual help and if we reject feminism, it must be for the right reason. That is not as part of a war between the sexes or tussle for superiority or power, all of which will only make matters worse. If we wish to do the right thing for the right reason then feminism must be rejected because of love.

If one can see why women might turn to feminism why should men pay it any attention? Could it be that any man who supports feminism actually lacks a real love for the feminine and the primary feminine virtues on the spiritual level of self-sacrifice, love, modesty, chastity, a nurturing nature, beauty and grace? How can he if he goes along with these qualities being trashed? But perhaps men follow the party line on this matter because they are weak, easily influenced by the zeitgeist or ideologically committed to the post-Enlightenment materialism which is the philosophical framework on which feminism is built. And then it cannot be ignored that Woman only began to stray from her natural role after Man betrayed his trust and was no longer focused on upholding the truth of God. His rebellion against God resulted in her rebellion against him. It was not a coincidence even if both could be seen as a form of self-assertion.

At any rate, no Christian man or woman for that matter can support feminism. I believe there are people who call themselves Christian feminists and even invent theologies to justify this aberration. You might as well talk about peaceful wars.

The metaphysical dynamic between the sexes on which the order of creation is built becomes easier to understand if you equate them to the vertical and horizontal polarities of existence. In general, men are more hierarchical and more interested in abstract thought while for women life is often more about relationships and maintaining the safety of the group. This is a very important part of life but it should not be the dominant force or society may descend into a prioritising of security over freedom.

I realise most people brought up in the modern world will not understand this and come up with all sorts of reasons why it is old-fashioned and repressive. The fact is, however, that they have an understanding based on limited information and are also most probably motivated by an unadmitted personal agenda. They will naturally accuse me and traditional thought of the same thing but ask yourself why it is only since we have lost sight of God that these ideas about equality of the sexes have arisen? When you lose contact with objective reality you have nothing left but human will and desire. Then you start to make your own reality and you can get away with this for a while but not forever. Sooner or later objective reality will reassert itself over your wishful thinking. I would speculate that in this case a forthcoming economic collapse might play a part in that.

I write about feminism in these pages because it sits squarely at the heart of the equality dogma and also because I see it as one of the great spiritual errors of the modern era, designed to attack humanity at its roots and reframe both men and women according to a materialistic agenda. Men and women are, and are meant to be, different and that difference is fundamental to the proper functioning of human society. It reflects the primal division of God and Nature which is echoed in the Christian idea of Christ as bridegroom and the Church as bride, and is the basis of expressed reality or creation. To attack that difference is to attack humanity and God who is the author of humanity.

The true nature of male and female and their complementary roles is something that goes down to a much deeper level of being than unaided reason can discern, though unprejudiced reason can easily find support for what is known at an instinctive or intuitive level. This is the level of first principles, things that just are and about which there can be no debate because what is, is. The reason that feminism has been able to make such inroads is because humanity is currently in a betwixt and between stage. It has grown out of instinct but not yet grown into intuition. Accordingly, it is stuck in a stage in which it relies on the intellectual/rational mind which is the stage when people are most separate from life and depend on their own mental resources to find their way. Those who are still living largely in instinct will automatically know the truth in this and other matters while those who have grown into the spiritual intuition will consciously know the truth.

But there are other factors too among which are egotism and resentment. For when the mind is under the sway of these, usually unacknowledged, ills, it will seek reasons to justify them. The unbalanced egotists behind feminism were pursuing simple self-advancement dressed up as equality. And modern women who identify as feminists are often doing what women do even more than men which is to follow the status quo. The men who go along with the programme do so out of an abdication of male leadership responsibility or else from a misplaced sense of fairness. Or a combination of these.

Feminism is a spiritual ill. This is not because it offers women a degree of personal autonomy but because it separates her from the mystery of her deeper being. It thereby cuts men off from that same mystery which they are often only able to perceive through her. As an anti-feminist I freely confess that women have a greater natural attunement to the spiritual world than men. But feminism makes a woman into an imitation man, in the process depriving her of her femininity. Of course, it can't really turn women into men but it does enough to deny them access to their true selves which was the intention. This was all part of the plan to isolate human beings in the material world and sever them from the spiritual.

Feminine nature when true to itself is oriented to a mystery beyond reason and pragmatism. This is not a romanticised male view of women. It is a fact. Something of this capacity should exist within all women but often it is undeveloped or tarnished by emotional reaction. Nevertheless, this is the basic truth at the core of the feminine mind. A typical masculine mind tends to go outwards and express itself actively while the feminine mind has a greater connection to the psychic world. The traditional wisdom of astrology conveys this idea with the signs of the zodiac, which are regarded as either positive or negative with the former, Aries, Leo etc., regarded as more extrovert and active while the latter, Cancer, Pisces and so on, are seen as more inwardly focused and more passive in their energy. We all have elements of both within ourselves but a woman's masculinity should always express itself within the fuller and dominating context of femininity, and vice versa.

How can we define this mystery? We can't. That's why it's a mystery. But we can say it is a spiritual quality that opens those who know it up to deeper truths than are available to the everyday mind. That is why things such as night, the moon and the sea are universally regarded as feminine. They contain mysteries. They don't show themselves openly and reveal everything clearly. Their truths are elusive but profound, and they feed the soul.

Mystery hides behind a veil. It has secrets. It is not for all to plumb its depths. Indeed, its depths can never be plumbed. This is a truth that lies at the core of mystery and makes it what it is. But something of it can be known, and its power is what lies behind creation. Mystery is, in this sense, the chaos, meaning formless potential rather than disorder, that is the fundamental material of creation, the stuff from which all things are made (cf. Jesus, *through* whom all things were made).

The book of Genesis is an important spiritual document in which profound wisdom is revealed in a simple, almost fairy tale manner. It presents man and woman as both made in the image of God but with different roles. Adam was created first but given a companion or helper to whom he was bound in love but who also he was intended to lead. That was his responsibility. Eve's role was to be a support to Adam, to do which effectively she was to be his spiritual equal. But the creation order was man then woman and that order was intended to be reflected in the natural order of being. There was to be a hierarchy. A hierarchy grounded in love but a hierarchy all the same. It is man and woman, husband and wife not the other way round. In love there is not superiority or inferiority but there is difference with each completing the other. If one half seeks to appropriate the ways of the other there is no completion and that means there can be no love in the fuller sense. Feminism has attacked the natural order of being and destroyed love. You might say that the natural order had not been functioning as it should and you would be right but you don't correct that by seeking to dismantle, or even reverse, the order.

Women who propagate feminism are setting themselves against truth. They are putting themselves on the side of the forces ranged against the good, against God in fact. This might be a hard saying for modern women to accept but that is because they have allowed their minds to be influenced by forces who do not wish their spiritual health. Traditionally civilisations have been formed by masculine energy and vision. Metaphorically speaking, they must be hewn out of rock. They are built through hard struggle and can only be preserved through hard struggle and the separation of higher and lower elements. When qualitative standards are reduced to be 'fair', meaning equal rather than just, decline rapidly sets in. All things break down and return to chaos unless one works to sustain them.

The feminine softens, balances and humanises the masculine. It keeps it from the destructiveness that is the other side of creativeness. But the creative impulse is masculine while the feminine is that which inspires creativity and when a culture no longer recognises this it will die. Feminine mystery is one of the chief causes of male creativity. When women turn away from this deeper aspect of their being, men lose a major part of their inspiration and their works turn more readily to evil. No feminist can ever be a real muse.

I don't blame women for feminism. At least I do blame a minority of women who were motivated by resentment and desire for power, but given the male rejection of God it was more or less inevitable. It is principally men who have created the conditions for this sickness of the modern mind with their chasing of spirit from the world. It is also undoubtedly true that if men had respected traditional feminine roles more and not treated women as inferiors, even chattels in some cultures, then women would not have felt the need for rebellion. The female reaction can be seen as largely in response to male behaviour and failure to live up to responsibility.

*

In Christianity God is Father, Son and Holy Spirit, a Trinity in which all three persons are masculine, the first two obviously so and the third it must be assumed so since it was through the power of the Holy Spirit that Mary became pregnant while Jesus himself uses the masculine pronoun when speaking of the Holy Spirit in the Gospel of St John. Does this mean there is no feminine aspect to God? Surely not. Femininity is one of the basic facts of existence, a primal fact. It must therefore be present in God. This does not alter the masculinity of the Creator (see the chapter I Am God) but must be considered in association with it.

The Divine Feminine can be seen in the context of creation as its womb or matrix, as Nature, *maya*, the phenomenal world itself, even space, but on the highest metaphysical level she might also be said to exist within the Triune Godhead. The Trinity is a trinity of persons. Persons are bound together by relationship and an essential part of relationship is receptivity. Between the three persons of the Trinity there is an ever-flowing relationship of love and within each one of these persons there must be receptivity to love. There is the giving and there is the receiving and this takes place eternally in the most fundamental part of the Trinity. The giving is the masculine side, the receiving, the feminine and we can visualise this as a constant and ceaseless outpouring and intaking between the three persons.

But there is more. Spiritual reality is made up of beings, persons not abstract qualities or impersonal energies and so this receptive aspect of God may also be conceived of as a being, a person. The Divine Feminine is thus she who enables love for you cannot have love without receptivity. Note that receptivity here is not the same thing as passivity, the latter being a purely negative quality that describes the state of being acted upon by an active force. Receptivity is a joyous, positive acceptance as can be found when one heart gives itself to another.

This is a suggestion of how the feminine can be present at the deepest, most existential, most intimate level of the Godhead without altering its essentially masculine nature that we know of from the scriptures, from the words of Jesus and from our own intuition. It is not introducing a fourth person to the Trinity but describing a process that takes place between the three persons. These are deep mysteries that we can only approach in the most clumsy and halting way but God invites us to contemplate his being since in the most profound way possible it is our own being too.

The Humanitarian God

I had a conversation a while ago with someone about religion but we came at the subject from radically different places. Hers was that religion is there to make the world a better place for all who live here. It exists to relieve suffering and make everybody happy and loving. Goodness lies in thinking of others, treating everyone equally and being kind. She actually thought this was the traditional Christian approach and when I pointed out that it could be shared by Christian and non-Christian alike, or even by believer and atheist, seemed a little nonplussed. But what's the point of religion if it brings nothing new to the table? Her attitude to spirituality encapsulates so much about the materialistic understanding of it, and is increasingly shared by many who consider themselves to be believers, but it shows a fundamental misunderstanding.

What is the purpose of religion? Is it to make people happy and comfortable in this world or is it to prepare them for the next? Is it to relieve suffering or is it to understand suffering? Now, obviously it is important to relieve suffering where one can but that is not the main issue from a spiritual perspective. Nothing I say here should be taken as refuting the simple fact that we should always seek to heal wounds when we are able to do so but there are deeper matters to consider. Relieving physical suffering is clearly a noble act but it should not be used as an excuse to obscure spiritual understanding.

If you believe in God, really believe in a spiritual God rather than simply follow a tradition, historical idea, set of ethics or the doctrines of an official religion, then you have a different attitude to the world and to human beings. Human beings then become not what they appear to be in the outward sense as phenomenal beings in everyday space and time but souls with a spiritual purpose in need of spiritual development. They are not just minds and bodies as we would ordinarily conceive them. They are spiritual beings and that puts them in an entirely different light. To fulfil them in the earthly sphere might have a detrimental spiritual impact. That does not mean you turn a blind eye to suffering but the real significance of life lies elsewhere. It is in developing first an awareness of and then a relationship with God and with God as a spiritual being, seeing yourself as a soul not the incarnated personality with needs and goals relating more to the former than the latter.

Most people live entirely in the world of appearance. They identify themselves with their outer being, their human body, emotions and thoughts, and when they think of God they think of him interacting with this person or saving this person. Even many religious people materialise spirituality in that they think the earthly human being is what matters. But the earthly human being is inherently and by default a sinner, that is to say, out of harmony with spiritual reality, and a sinner can only be saved by renouncing his sins and not just his sins but his identification with himself as an earthly human being. The earthly human being can never get to heaven. This needs to be understood. You only get to heaven and so fulfil your divine purpose and destiny by transferring the focus of your being from the earthly self to the spiritual soul. If you don't know what this means you are a materialist whatever your beliefs.

God is not a humanitarian. Certainly not in the sense we normally understand the meaning of this word. That is because although he loves the whole human being there is a hierarchical dimension to this love and he loves the soul more than the body. This is not to discount the body but to put things in perspective. It is good to feed and to heal the body but not at the expense of the soul and if the focus on the body is used to obscure the reality and prior claim of the soul then you are not acting in a godly fashion. It is hard to escape the sense that in recent times the humanitarian impulse, in itself a noble impulse, has been twisted and is being used to advance an attack on deeper spiritual values.

The pre-eminent spiritual quality is love of God. That should go without saying since Jesus said it. But for the follower of the humanitarian God the New Testament is reduced to the parable of the Good Samaritan with other, more important teachings such as the love of God, the recognition of Christ, the rejection of the world and the fact of good and evil as spiritual realities ignored. To love one's neighbour is certainly a commandment but it comes after the commandment to love God and, properly speaking, is dependent on it which tells us that love of the neighbour means acting for his spiritual good, doing what will bring him closer to God. Love always means working for spiritual good. If you think you love your neighbour but use that supposed love to solidify him in his sins you are not responding to real love at all but something that comes from you rather than from God.

It's worth looking at how Jesus behaved to get a fuller understanding of this. He healed the sick but why did he do this? After all he healed some people but not all, and he fed the 5,000 that one time but not every day. Everything Jesus did served his primary purpose which was to impart spiritual understanding and by that I mean the understanding of the higher world and the after death destiny of those who followed him. Jesus was not concerned with being an altruist in this world but with guiding human beings towards the next. All his miracles were intended to point to the reality of heaven. When he healed the body, he was really trying to awaken the soul.

Linked to this erroneous idea of the spiritual as being about social improvement is a similar one of the spiritual as being about self-improvement. A spirituality that is focused on human beings and their spiritual development rather than on God is common nowadays. It generally fits right in with the egalitarian humanism of the contemporary world, simply adding a spiritual patina to that. It seeks personal benefit here and now in the form of an increased sense of well-being and peace rather than to put the soul right with God on his terms and irrespective of what that might bring as regards pain and suffering to the individual. It is really a form of psychological therapy rather than true religion.

The word sacrifice means to make holy and is etymologically related to sacred. Humanistic spirituality is not sacrificial but sacrilegious in that it attempts to steal sacred things that by right belong to God and appropriate them by the self on the human level. It pursues the religious path for what it can get from it, from wanting heaven rather than loving God but heaven *is* the love of God not the desire for his gifts. This false motive corrupts the entire spiritual approach so even if such a person engages in traditional spiritual practices such as prayer or meditation or ritual of whatever sort the work is tainted. This does not mean it won't bring results or that the results may not seem to them to be authentic spiritual experiences, but they will be empty of real spiritual benefit and merely feed the ego.

The desire for spiritual experience is understandable but should quickly be outgrown. We do not come to Earth to have spiritual experiences but to learn and so, generally speaking, such experiences will come to the seeker at the beginning of his journey to give him encouragement and the sense that what he aspires to really does exist but thereafter he may not be favoured. To seek to repeat past experiences is the sign of a spiritual sensualist.

Human-centred spirituality is actually an aspect of materialism. It is the spirituality of the materialist, a person whose whole mindset is formed by materialism and whose motivations relate to the earthly self and the satisfaction of its goals and desires but who has simply broadened his horizons to include a wider range of experiences. He is seeking to be fed and wants to bring the spiritual down to his soul rather than take his soul up to the spiritual. The first commandment will always be to love God with all your heart and all your mind and all your soul. A human-centred spirituality is a spirituality of this world. A humanitarian God is a false god and if you follow such a God, you will not progress beyond the material world.

Ideology and Freedom

We have pointed out the fallacy of the all men are created equal dogma which underlies much contemporary materialistic ideology. This might have arisen in the normal course of events as society changed and evolved, and technological development facilitated the establishment of an egalitarian ethos, but I would contend that it was also deliberately fostered as a means of dismantling the traditional values of Western civilisation centred in the reality of God and the truth of creation. I say Western because that is where the attack has been focused but it is a global project that will encompass all traditional forms of belief which will either be assimilated (Westernised Buddhism appears to be particularly easy in this regard and Islam particularly difficult) or destroyed.

Many fashionable ideologies of the moment derive from a materialistic approach to life and are used to bring down real spiritual values which are based on a vertical (qualitative and hierarchical) approach to reality rather than a horizontal (quantitative and egalitarian) one. Note that the horizontal is not here denied but regarded as subordinate to the vertical which is primary.

Add to these ideologies measures taken to contain climate change and the recent coronavirus infection and you have the framework of a universal system based on atheistic materialism which is used to control mankind and separate human beings from their spiritual source, locking them firmly in this world with no avenue of escape. In this system no true freedom of thought is allowed. Everything and everyone must be brought into the fold, submit to the ideology and conform to the agenda. The only religions tolerated will be those that allow themselves to be spiritually emasculated as so much contemporary Christianity has done when it accommodates itself to the world.

The System will be universal, global, unquestionable and without exit or escape. It will be the iron prison of group think in which the good is redefined to mean worldly good, the soul denied and the Creator chased from creation.

The approach to the issues of today should not be reduced to a left/right culture war. That idea is a distraction and a diversion. This is nothing less than a spiritual battle for human souls. So, make sure you pick the right side. Trust your intuition and don't be misled by power and authority in any form. There will be many false goods dangled before your eyes. To go along with these will be presented as the mark of a good person. Reject them and you are a sinner according to contemporary ideology. But that ideology is based on a mistaken idea of what man is and if you are true to your divine source, you should know this. How do you attune yourself to this divine source? God presents himself to us in Nature (the Creation which is not perfect in this world but has enough perfection in it to show its source), in Scripture (which should call forth an intuitive response in the rightly oriented) and in your own heart. None of these are perfect but that is as it should be because personal discernment is always required for a self-conscious being who is supposed to grow into a god. At the same time, they do all contain more than enough to guide us to reality if we will allow it. Learn from this threefold approach to see the truth and free yourself from the lies of the modern world.

We supposedly live in a humanistic age, one in which mankind is central and owes nothing to anything or indeed anyone beyond itself. We are our own justification. We celebrate ourselves, and our art, politics and science are all based on expanding our knowledge and deepening our fulfilment of ourselves as ourselves. For some our potential is limitless but it is still our potential as human beings even if we bring the universe into it on some abstract or quasi-spiritual level.

What we don't realise is that humanity restricted to humanity is doomed to a solipsistic nihilism, however much we may give our fundamental emptiness a false glamour. The human being can only find any real fulfilment when it goes beyond itself. In fact, the human being is only properly human when it understands itself to be more than human. Humanism really means separation from God so it is an anti-spiritual philosophy. Truth to tell, it is an anti-human philosophy because the human being without God is destined for death.

We don't live in a humanistic age. We live in an inhuman age. We cover up that grim reality with technological distractions and false ideas about ourself. We are lost, on our own, floating off into the void. We are so insane that the only people who aware of this are regarded as mad or childish because they supposedly cling onto fantasies. But the biggest fantasy and the greatest arrogance is that we can live without God. Remove the artificial supports that modern human beings have, take away the elaborate structures we have built up to keep out reality and most people might reflect a little more deeply on what they are and what they should be.

The ground is being prepared for the incarnation of a being known as the Antichrist by Christians who is probably the same as the one named Ahriman by the spiritual philosopher Rudolf Steiner. This is that aspect of evil which seeks to bind human beings to the material world and cut them off completely from the spiritual. The advent of this being has been prepared by our reduction of life to what can be weighed and measured. Our modern arts, sciences, politics and philosophy and even medicine have all been pressed into service to accommodate the ends of this individual. Computer technology serves his purposes very well. Even religion when it focuses more on humanitarianism than true spirituality starts to become the servant of Antichrist/Ahriman. When he appears, he will not be obviously evil like some of the despots of the twentieth century. He may even appear benign by the materialistic standards we have built up over the last couple of centuries. But he will seek to divert us from true divine understanding and spiritual life. We need to understand that anything or anyone that promises happiness and fulfilment in this world, whatever it calls itself, is not of God. That doesn't mean that hardship and suffering are good in themselves. That also can be a false path. But this life is intended to serve the greater life and can never be justified in itself.

The current state of the world has been brought about to make us ripe for the picking when the Antichrist arrives, but God has not abandoned us. If we can see through the lies, we become spiritually stronger. The lies are permitted because they must be brought out into the open in order for us to overcome them and that which corresponds to them in our own souls. If they were not made manifest and outwardly present in this way, we would not be able to defeat them and nor could we deal with the same tendencies that exist within ourselves. There is risk involved. The darkness can overwhelm us or we can use it to see the light more clearly. But we are, or should be, spiritual adults now and we can only progress spiritually by facing reality and dealing with it. God will protect us but he will not overprotect us for then we would never grow up.

Ahriman/Antichrist has many servants in the modern world, most of whom don't know they are his servants even though they serve his agenda and prepare his way. I would go so far as to say that more or less anyone in the public eye who has any form of power serves his agenda. If they didn't, they wouldn't be there. This will only become more so. The plans are laid for complete control of human consciousness. That's not just control of human beings but control of human consciousness. The best slaves are willing slaves and that is what Ahriman wants and what his agents are currently working for in preparation for his appearance. We have to be aware of this. Preserve your freedom. God gave us complete freedom, making us free even to reject him. No one and nothing can take that away but you can give it away. Never sell your birthright, no matter what is offered in exchange for whatever is offered is worthless in comparison. Stay free.

How does all this relate to equality, the subject of this book? It's simple really. The attempt to establish the equality idea has to do with enforcing compliancy and stopping people thinking for themselves. It is to create a herd mentality with everyone thinking in the same way, a way that is controlled by the powers that be. You can have equality or freedom. You can't have both. This is the battle of our time. On one side is God and freedom. On the other, spiritual slavery hiding behind the delusionary offer of an end to suffering.

A Vulgar Age

Some thirty years ago my spiritual teachers told me that we were living during a period of greater vulgarity than at any time during the history of our planet. Things could hardly be said to have improved since then. Assuming they knew what they were talking about it, as I do and it's not hard to tell from contemporary culture anyway, what might be the cause of this vulgarity?

In one respect it can be linked to the decline of traditional aristocratic values and the rise of democracy with its belief that all men are equal. Sometimes the equality idea is viewed as a consequence of Christianity with its focus on the meek and humble but it took over 1,700 years to appear so that can't be the only explanation if it is any explanation at all. The misinterpretation of a thing is not the thing itself and it is telling that this presumed result of Christianity only arose after Christianity ceased to be a significant factor in the lives of most Western men and women. It was therefore not the result of Christianity so much as the decline and fall of Christianity. It appeared from the ashes of Christianity as the spiritual content of the religion was lost, leaving behind just its material form. It is the residue of a Christianity that was separated from heaven and relocated to reside in this world.

Everything must be seen in context and the Christian emphasis on the lowly can be understood in terms of a society in which hierarchy had degenerated as it will tend to do in a fallen world. Praising the humble was not to exalt the lesser over the greater but to assert the importance of each individual human being, something that had not been properly acknowledged before. It was also there to teach humility and as a means of subduing the recalcitrant ego which must be brought into line before the soul can enter heaven.

However, hierarchy still exists in heaven. Christ is king. He is envisaged as sitting on a throne. His angels are ranged in ranks according to their station. The Christian attention to the humble only meant that we should focus on spiritual hierarchy rather than worldly status. The poor are not spiritually superior to the rich by virtue of being poor but those with earthly riches are certainly not, on that account, spiritually superior to the poor either and they may be subject to greater temptations. At the same time, if the rich might be tempted to succumb to pride because of their riches so the poor may fall prey to the similarly soul-sapping vice of envy.

Democracy came about because a substantial proportion of human beings had reached a certain stage in their evolution. A certain intellectual stage and a certain stage in their development as individuals with autonomy. They could no longer just be subject to an authority over which they had no control or a power which ruled them whether they consented to this or not. They had earned the right to have a say in their governance. This is similar to the stage of late adolescence and any parent knows what a difficult and challenging time that can be. A time of rebellion when mistakes are often made as the child starts to become an adult. It is a necessary stage but one fraught with potential problems.

And it seems that problems have arisen. The rebellious teenager has not grown up. Adolescence should be a relatively short phase in the transition from childhood to adulthood but we appear to have fallen into a period of arrested adolescence. Instead of coming out the other side with a new-found maturity and joining the adult (for which read spiritual) world as full members, we have plunged more deeply into adolescence and unharnessed self-will. As a consequence of that we have lost touch with the spiritual completely, and the spiritual is the adult. It is a higher stage of being, a more mature stage into which we should have grown bringing to it our newly developed sense of self, brought to the fore by its experiences in matter wherein it was separated from God and so had to make its own path.

Democracy may have been called for by this greater sense of self-consciousness in the masses but as more people moved into this stage, and thereby influenced the culture, they brought down its quality, hitherto largely determined by an elite. Standards were lowered hence the vulgarity, a word whose original meaning refers to the common people or masses. We live in a vulgar age because we live in a democratic age but it may be we have to experience that in order to go beyond it. That is one scenario. Another would be that the trend continues on a downwards trajectory. That, of course, was Plato's view when he predicted that democracy creates disorder in both the individual and society as a whole because of its tendency to make liberty licence and so it must end in tyranny. We are back to the way being paved for the Antichrist.

According to traditional metaphysics our vulgar age was inevitable. In many ancient cosmologies, time was regarded as flowing in cycles with a primeval Golden Age when man walks with the gods descending to a spiritually darkened time in which matter becomes more dense and impenetrable and consciousness collapses in on itself. Then the process concludes in cosmic destruction and a new era commences with another Golden Age. We have alluded to this idea previously.

Christianity replaced it with a new understanding in which time progresses in a linear fashion from creation in the Garden of Eden leading eventually through a historical process to the city of the New Jerusalem in which creation is transformed and drawn up into divine reality.

Many people in the spiritual world today reject the Christian view and prefer the cyclical one, seeing it as making more metaphysical sense. Strangely enough, one approach that roughly mirrors the Christian idea is the modern materialistic understanding of human life which would maintain we are progressing to a better human form in which science and technology correct all the faults of nature and give us, if not immortality, at least a more perfect vehicle to house our consciousness which will also be tweaked and improved through technological means whether that be drugs or even by blending us with machines. This is transhumanism, a great spiritual evil because it denies the spirit replacing it entirely with matter, but one to which the modern world seems to be tending.

Which of these two ideas about time is the more accurate? My contention would be that there are elements of truth in both. Time is indeed cyclical and the notion of a Golden Age when the veil between spirit and matter was thin, gradually descending to a time when spirit is withdrawn and the material world becomes more present until it is all that is present, is correct. Certain powers such as clairvoyance are lost in order for other faculties, chiefly reason and the intellect, to develop which they can only do with a more constricted consciousness. But time also moves forward in a historical sense and if there is a spiritual descent it has an evolutionary purpose which is to bring about the conditions in which consciousness can become more individualised with a greater sense of personal freedom in the darkened material conditions. Then there can be a reascent but with the fruits of greater self-awareness. This is how men can become gods.

Many people interested in traditionalist metaphysics believe that all religions convey the same essential truths. There is a perennial philosophy which is the root of them all and they differ only in externals and certain relatively unimportant doctrines. I disagree. There is something qualitatively different about Christianity and what Christ brought to human consciousness. It has to do with freedom, it has to do with love and it has to do with time. In traditional metaphysics time is something to be transcended. One goes beyond all aspects of the material to enter into spiritual consciousness. But Christ redeemed creation which means the qualities of the relative world are not wholly transcended and effectively lost but they are spiritualised and so add something to divine reality, something that was not there before.

Time is certainly a great mystery in that there is a pristine state beyond earthly time which is the state of divine being. However, time is not simply an illusion from the spiritual point of view. It is not just swallowed up in eternity. Through time creation is brought to fulfilment but then at the end of worldly time something happens that is similar to what happened to Christ's body at the Ascension. Time will be taken up into eternity which it will thereby enrich. To changelessness will have been added the capacity to grow and become more, and this is the gift of time. It is the dynamic element in eternity.

Equality and vulgarity go together. We may not wish to acknowledge this long known truism because it offends our modern sensibilities but the levelling down process that is egalitarianism has an inevitable effect. Standards fall. One can imagine a state in which this might not happen but that would presuppose a high general level of spiritual evolution. I don't imagine even the most ardent partisans for equality would claim that is the case now.

End Times

In Christian tradition the End Times is that period when humanity is judged. Other traditions, most notably the Indian, also speak of a period when true spiritual understanding is lost and mankind has descended into materialism and ignorance. It is that time when we have gone so far away from the source that we have not only lost contact with it but even deny that it exists. We redefine good and evil to mean what brings happiness or removes suffering in the physical world with no thought of the spiritual. There is no longer an absolute reality that can serve as the bedrock of moral being. As a result, the centre constantly shifts until there is no real centre at all and we behave with increasing individualism. Traditional values are first rejected and then inverted. Goodness is hard to find and wickedness abounds though it is not generally recognised as such because how do you recognise spiritual wickedness at a time which denies the reality of spirit? This Kali Yuga as it is known in Indian metaphysics is none other than the vulgar age of which we have just spoken. Equality is one of its hallmarks since the imposition of equality eradicates the difference between higher and lower, leading to the dominance of the lower by simple fact of numerical superiority.

There are several indicators that we are in the End Times now. The first and most obvious is that we live in a world in which materialism and atheism are the default assumptions. More and more, as has been proved over the last few years, even religion submits itself to the materialistic diktats. Religious belief is allowed only when it doesn't interfere with what is actually supposed to matter. Most children grow up today with no awareness of any spiritual tradition. If they do know of anything like that it's often just quaint and irrelevant to so-called real life. Christianity, as was predicted, has been chased to the periphery, a hangover from the past which may be admired for its humanistic qualities but has no spiritual significance.

That would suffice by itself to prove we are in the End Times but there are other clear signs this is so. One not mentioned in prophecy as far as I am aware, but highly significant, is that the population of the world has expanded to unprecedented levels. It makes perfect sense that at a time of mass testing and gathering in, a separation of sheep and goats, a large number of souls would be present. This is a point of culmination and many souls would either wish to be present or else are required to be so for an examination of their spiritual polarisation. Souls of all degrees are being asked fundamental questions and their response will have a bearing on their future existence. It is as though we have taken the course and are now being tested on what we have learnt. Most people don't know they are being tested but that is part of the test. Our ignorance brings about an involuntary honesty in our response.

As the End Times is a summing up of an entire cycle, we find that all the past has now become present in a certain form. We have access to previous ages in a way that has never before been possible. Anyone in any part of the world can acquaint himself with the knowledge and culture of all historical civilisations. Everything is being swept up and brought into this grand culminating moment. It may well be that the enormous population increase of the last few decades is because many souls who incarnated during the age that is coming to a close have been summoned to appear before the court. It's a time of reckoning and everything that existed in whatever form has been gathered up and brought into the here and now. Previously these souls may have inclined to a spiritual belief because all cultures did so and therefore it was imposed on them from outside. Now they have to show whether they have an inclination towards the spiritual when the culture denies it, and if they do have such, how is that demonstrated? Is it at the centre of their lives or just a spiritual gloss on still materialistic thought patterns?

The End Times were predicted and they were predictable because they are an inevitable result of entropy. At the beginning of a cycle a great infusion of spiritual energy is injected into the world. It is this infusion that makes the Golden Age that all traditions speak of as having existed at the beginning of time. After that there is a continual dropping off of truth and righteousness until these things have almost entirely disappeared. That time is now. Of course, as the spiritual energy dissipates there is a compensatory response on the material level and that is why we have reached such heights of technology and material well-being, factors which enable the great increase in population. But this material progress masks and also contributes to the spiritual decline and the latter has now reached such proportions as to lead one to the conclusion that a significant point is at hand.

The dominance of technology in today's world is a further factor that points to the End Times. We are dependent on it in every aspect of our lives, but here's the problem. Technology separates us from the spiritual and from the natural. We are so foolish as to celebrate that and even to seriously consider augmenting our being with technology, in effect turning ourselves into machines. For advocates of this diabolical practice, it is just a development from a person wearing a pair of glasses but there is a line which we appear shortly about to cross, one in which the technological/mechanical will dominate, and if we do cross that line, we will lose our humanity. I suspect that for many this may already have started to happen and when it happens on a large scale the world will be completely cut off from the spiritual at which point it will start to collapse. It is the spiritual that gives life. When that has gone, existence can only be maintained by stealing life from elsewhere which means other beings on which the thief becomes parasitical. In a world that has given itself over to technology in the extreme sense I am talking about the stronger will maintain themselves by feeding off the weaker. That is the world of hell. In the Golden Age there was no technology because there was no need for it. I am not saying all technology is evil but it has a tendency to become so and it has become so now. We are called to be creative and yet this should always be within the bounds of spiritual understanding and certainly never work against it.

The End Times have arrived. This is only the beginning of the End Times period and it may stretch out for a long while yet so the fact that we are in them does not mean that there is not some distance still to go. Only God knows. Nonetheless, it makes sense to observe the signs. Watch and pray remains the best advice for these days as they may grow increasingly dark.

But there is another side to this coin and that is that in many respects it is a real privilege to be alive now. By resisting the downward pull, we can make a great leap forward in our spiritual unfoldment. These days if you are to be spiritually focused you must make an active effort to be so. Society will not help you go in that direction. You must swim against the tide and the current is strong. However, this will develop your spiritual muscles. Now you have the opportunity of a lifetime or perhaps one should say of lifetimes.

The objection might be raised that people have always said that the end of the world is nigh. Even the first Christians thought they were living in the final days. That is quite true but there are several differences between now and the past. Firstly, there has never been a time when the spiritual decadence was global. Always there have been some areas that were relatively untouched by the general malaise whether that be during the time of the Roman Empire or at other times when dominant cultures and civilisations had peaked, become corrupt and were declining. Certain groups carried the potential for recovery. Not now. Spiritual loss has spread throughout the entire world.

Materialism and atheism are everywhere, in every nation, and they are the default in all classes. The inversion of values has never been so universal, the erosion of the difference between men and women a powerful example. Technology now has the power to separate us from nature as well as God. This has not happened before and certainly not to the same extent and universally. These times really are unprecedented.

Technology Is Not Neutral

Some people believe you can have science or God but not both. I understand this point of view and yet science is just a word for knowledge. Surely it is not wrong to explore the creation as long as one does it while fully acknowledging the Creator and seeing everything in his light? Perhaps the problem is that science easily corrupts the scientist and the type of person who becomes a scientist is often (not always) a materialist who lacks both imagination and intuition not to mention faith. Maybe the scientific method and way of thinking actually require one to close off parts of one's mind that are spiritually attuned or to atrophy these parts.

Having sounded a precautionary note, I would like to explore the possibility that there is indeed a conflict between science and God. Here are some thoughts put forward for consideration. They fly in the face of contemporary wisdom but that is a good thing if it makes us look at the subject afresh.

What if our modern science and technology, especially the latter, actually derive from a highly intelligent but spiritually dead demonic source and is given to humanity to separate us from God and bring about our spiritual corruption?

The stories we hear about scientists being inspired in dreams which are sometimes taken as being somehow divine in origin may be something quite other. The spiritual and the demonic are often confused by those who have no experience of such things.

What brought about the Fall of Man from Paradise? It was when the serpent promised Eve that she could be the equal of Adam and even God if she ate from the Tree of Knowledge of Good and Evil. Now, this tree and its fruit were presumably created by God so were not bad in themselves but the sin was to eat from the tree before being ready and against the specific instruction from God not to do so. The fruit represents the mind or thought which are not bad things except when they are separated from the spiritual source and regarded as independent of God. That is our contemporary science, is it not?

Eating the fruit means awakening to mind and the world of opposites it reveals and that in turn brings about the sense of a separate self. It destroyed Paradise and resulted in the Fall. Sin and death entered the world and they entered, it could reasonably be said, with science. Just to repeat. The problem here is not mind but mind divorced from soul and spirit.

The process has continued. Over the last 300 years technology put through from demonic levels has destroyed tradition and religion and turned the world into an outpost of hell. You have only to look at our art and architecture to see that. Technology has corrupted our minds and now, with the diabolical fantasies of transhumanism, is even beginning to deform the human image. The Faustian pact gives us power over our world and our outer self but at the price of severing the link with the divine and our true being.

We get material power but each new form of technology takes us further away from God and the soul. We accept this happily because we only see the benefits which are not even benefits really because they soon pall and we demand more like a junkie with his fix.

Technology is about replacing man with machine, first externally but increasingly internally. Depending on machines for everything just makes our consciousness more mechanical and less alive which is why everything is duller these days. Our minds and our very consciousness become desensitised by technology and they shrivel. The computers we increasingly live our lives through are stealing our souls and eroding our spiritual faculties which range from imagination to awareness of the sacred. Even our moral sense is undermined.

Where is all this leading? Is the aim to turn this world into hell and human beings into soulless zombies which the demons can exploit for their own ends? That may be why they wish to have people mentally and physically remade by technology. It is like the corruption of elves into orcs by Morgoth in Tolkien's legendarium. But perhaps the technological advancements have another aim as well.

Demons lack bodies. They have lost their angelic forms and do not have a physical form either. They are spirits in the inner dimensions but they crave form for the greater powers of self-expression and freedom this would give them. Is it possible that through technology, through computers, through artificial intelligence, they are trying to gain an entry into this world? Could this provide the platform they need to incarnate directly in matter? Remember they are currently neither in spirit proper nor matter. They exist in a kind of limbo world, cut off from God. By remodelling the physical world so it is no longer the natural creation, they make it possible to connect directly with it. Through digital and mechanical means they can incarnate. Sensitive souls have complained about the spiritual ravages caused by the Industrial Revolution from the beginning. Blake and Wordsworth were at the forefront of this but we have ignored them because we are so easily seduced by material goods. But now things are much worse. The dream of freedom offered by technology is close to becoming the nightmare of slavery to it.

From the normal point of view this interpretation of what lies behind science and technology is crazy, the stuff of science fiction as the saying goes. But maybe science fiction can warn us of what may happen if we let it. No, what will happen if we do not take active steps to stop it. We absolutely must rediscover God and reject completely the lure of the demons before they destroy us. Could this be what happened before and brought about the necessity for God to drown a previous humanity at the time of the Flood? For one thing is certain. Even if the demons succeed their success won't last long. God will not permit it.

Surely they know that? Perhaps, but maybe their pride thinks they can get away with it this time. It's up to us to make sure they do not.

Even if we forget about the demons, can anyone deny the nefarious influence of modern technology on the soul or, better put, on awareness of the soul? It should be self-evident that our technology sprang from and promotes the materialistic mindset. Stone Age man had tools but that was different. A line is crossed when the technology we use is no longer made by hand and the average person cannot understand how it is made. Then we find we have separated ourselves from the world of spirit and embedded ourselves deeply in matter. That is why it is a mistake to say that technology is neutral, it's how we use it that matters. The kind of technology we have inevitably bends our mind into a shape that accommodates itself to it. The more sophisticated the technology, the more it separates us from God. The only way to protect against this is to be very aware of it.

Technology cannot be neutral because it makes expectations of us. It forces us to act and to think in a certain way. The technology we use determines the sort of people we become. A materialistic technology makes a materialistic people. It must do this because it makes assumptions about life that we tacitly absorb when we use it. Over time it even moulds our minds into a form that is congenial to it.

The technology we use profoundly affects our relationship with the world and our approach to God so it isn't what we do with it that matters. It does things with us, with us and to us, and a materialistic technology will materialise our minds. It desanctifies the world and dehumanises us because it separates us from both God and Nature. That is what it has already done and the process increases by the day.

I am quite aware that I can be accused of hypocrisy in saying this because I use technology when I criticise the basis of it, but I live in the modern world and have to adjust to it up to a point.

That doesn't mean that I can't envisage a situation better than the one we have. Do you not know that if our consciousness changed, the world would also change? A spiritualised consciousness would produce a more spiritualised world. The physical environment would actually adapt to our minds. We cannot use the tools of materialism without materialising ourselves.

Since 2020 it has become obvious that the world is well on the way to being ruled by a system of technocracy. Politics and politicians play their part but they are increasingly just enacting the will of a group of technical specialists and experts working to impose control over the populace. In their own minds and according to their own beliefs, these people may be well-motivated and working for the good of humanity but that is because their vision of life has been corrupted. They are completely materialistic, regarding human beings as things to be worked on. Certainly, to be brought to an optimum level of efficiency, at once intellectual, emotional and moral, and made collectively happy with suffering, both physical and mental, reduced to a minimum, but ultimately little more than machines which need effective servicing to run smoothly. In this scenario, the individual is of diminished importance, personal freedom is allowed only to the extent that it doesn't interfere with the overall programme and the spiritual is completely denied except insofar as a pseudo-spiritual might be included as a psychological palliative.

It is computer technology that has made this possible. There are grounds for saying that computers are one of the greatest disasters to have befallen human beings since we got thrown out of Eden. So seductive that we have all succumbed to them but in reality. separating us from the soul more than we ever have been because in some ways they parody true spiritual consciousness. Indeed, computers can be regarded as a material perversion of the spiritual in that they externalise on a lower level and in a degraded fashion some of the qualities of the soul thus disincentivising us to seek the higher reality. But they have also laid bare the myth that technology in itself is neutral. Because our minds adopt the form of the technology we use, we are starting to think like computers and in terms of computer technology. In so doing we create a solid wall between our conscious minds and higher domains of spiritual freedom and intuition.

Technocracy is anti-God because it is materialistic, atheistic, seeks complete control, subordinates truth to the expedient and the efficient, denies the primacy of the good, the beautiful and the true and puts power in the hands of an unaccountable few whose expertise in specialised areas blinds them to the overall picture. But for the technocratic type of mind, theirs is the best way to organise society because this mind is oblivious to what lies beyond the quantitative level.

In a world controlled by data and spreadsheets there is no room for beauty, mystery, sacrifice or love. It is a world run by algorithms in which neither freedom nor the real good can find expression, good now being defined as that which makes the system run more efficiently. Human beings are viewed in terms of their material selves only, and this in a far more complete way than any of our previous political systems which were a hotchpotch of the natural human and materialistic ways of thinking. Technocracy is materialism brought to full power and complete dominance. It is the logical conclusion of materialism hence its appeal to materialistic minds. There is no space for anything outside a closed system. Inevitably, any technocracy will collapse in the long run because there cannot be a closed system. Truth must eventually interpose. However, tremendous damage can be done to the soul before this position is reached.

If hell can be defined as a place closed to divine influence, then the ideal technocratic society is a reasonable image of one kind of hell, the kind run by measurement and numbers in which all is controlled and predictable and the soul is a known quantity. And this is what we are in the process of constructing. It's what the events of the last few years have brought closer. The question is, do you want your soul to be just a statistic on a computer?

I Am God

The first temptation to equality came in the Garden of Eden which we may understand as a true myth meaning not literally true but symbolically accurate as a description of the development of human consciousness. This was when the snake or Satan or the principle that works against God, call it what you will, tempted the human being to seek to be the equal of God. Right from the beginning there was the appeal to envy and the justification of sin. Eve was disobeying God but the fruit of the tree was good for food and pleasing to the eye. Another less remarked upon aspect about the desire for equality is that it masks a desire for superiority. This may have its roots in the right and proper desire of the self for progress and development but it becomes perverted by the ego wanting these things in its own time and on its own terms.

In this chapter I would like to address a common spiritual misunderstanding. Common, at least, among those who have moved somewhat beyond conventional religion, meaning religion as an external body of beliefs, into the more mystical idea that God dwells within us and can be known directly, but not far enough to see how he dwells within us and in what way he can be known. This is all one with many forms of Eastern mysticism. I am God. You are God. We are all God. Everyone is God. Everything is God.

In point of fact, this is true but only up to a point. God is indeed within every bit of his creation which could not be unless he was so present, but he is also transcendent to it and his transcendence ontologically precedes his immanence. Put another way, he is immanent in part but transcendent *in toto*.

I want to keep this simple and not go into elaborate differences between pantheism and panentheism. I will leave that for the philosophers but I will say this. God is in everything but at different degrees of closeness. For Christians he is fully in Jesus but he is in everyone. However, you can only know him to the degree that a), you have opened up to him – this is faith or acceptance, and b), you are able to manifest him. A pint pot cannot contain a gallon of liquid let alone a whole ocean full. And the ocean that is God is infinitely large.

Therefore, while I may be God if I am fully transparent to him through faith (not belief, you can believe in anything but faith is intuitive recognition of spiritual reality) and a wholly purified soul, even then I am not God as God is God. I don't begin to approach that. God may be in his creation but he stands outside it in his fullness and no created being can ever know the wholeness of God. What that being can do is become attuned to God and thereby become godlike, and from that initial stage become ever more aware of the unplumbable depths of God. But he can never be God.

The mystical forms of religion and esotericism, both East and West, that identify the soul with God are not wholly wrong but nor are they wholly right. They mistake a star for the source of light. It is, forgive me for saying this, the error of the spiritual beginner. Or else, and forgive those who succumb to this, it is Satanic inflation. I am God and you are God insofar as God dwells within us and can be known as the ground of our being. But I, William Wildblood, am not God and never will be in the whole of eternity. I may eventually grow so far into God as to be able to wield godlike powers, as may you, but that is an entirely different matter. The gap between created and Creator can be bridged but it can never be completely overcome.

Ultimate reality is seen by some mystical schools of thought as pure being and if that were indeed the case and monism a fact then an enlightened soul could say with perfect justification 'I am God'. In this scenario there would be no more personal I. There would only be the realisation of absolute 'I-ness'. I am God because my personal I has been absorbed by the universal

I, absorbed and effectively destroyed. However, if ultimate reality resides not in abstract being but in a concrete Person the situation is different. Then my personal I is not absorbed but made one with God who is not just being (he is that too) but *a* being, the living God. In this scenario, the individual soul is made one with universal spirit but retains full individuality. He can say 'I am one with God' but he will not say 'I am God'. Only in this case is there room for love because love is between persons. In monism or non-duality (there is a difference but it is somewhat academic), love from an ultimate point of view would be an illusion of the unenlightened. However, that is reductive because it dismisses creation as ultimately surplus to requirements, without meaning or truth, whereas the personal God incorporates all the beauty of creation and plurality into eventual oneness.

The great achievement of the West, culminating over the last 500 years, has been the creation of the full individual. In no other culture anywhere in the world has the individual had any real value, and although there are tributaries feeding into this river from classical times, notably from Greece, its real source can be regarded as Christianity and specifically Christ, the God who became Man and was at once fully human and fully divine. The philosophical, intellectual and spiritual underpinning of the importance of the individual was rooted in the Christian concept of the person.

It is sometimes said that Man adds nothing to God. God is the Absolute, the infinite and the eternal to which nothing can be added and from which nothing can be taken away. And yet, if that were the case, why creation? But let's not reduce God to a mathematical concept or an abstraction. He is the Living God and he is Love. We say he because the Creator God is the impregnating spirit that gives life and form to matter. He stands outside creation which is generated by him not incubated in him, and all creation is receptive, i.e., feminine, to him. This does not mean there is no feminine aspect of the divine and that it is not fundamental meaning primordial but this would correspond to Cosmic Womb or universal substance rather than inspiring or animating spirit. He is Spirit, she is the principle or essence of Matter and the ground of creation, Mater or Mother.

God is a person and we are made in the image of God. What is a person? It is a free individual, not reducible to anything else. Many religions discount the idea of freedom and that of the individual, seeing man as either nothing in relation to God (Islam) or part of God in a way that completely emphasises the divine over the human (most Eastern religions). Only in Christianity, the religion in which God became man, are the individual and his intrinsic freedom truly valued. In this way, man, each individual man and woman, can add something to the spiritual life of the universe and therefore to God himself once they realign themselves with divine being. Our God-realised individual self makes the universe a richer, more creation filled place whereas in monistic conceptions of life all the billions of human souls add nothing to the universe. They leave it as they found it. That's rather pointless, isn't it?

*

I said above that the realisation of full individuality is an achievement of the West and derives from the Christian idea of the person, and that is the case. But did you know that the only language in which the first person singular pronoun is capitalised is English? I only learned this recently and haven't confirmed it but, according to my limited knowledge of other languages (*je, ich, yo, io, ego*), it appears to be true. It undoubtedly has some significance, reinforced by the fact that the letter 'I' is like the numeral 1.

The significance, as I see it, is that the English-speaking peoples were those who were most conscious of themselves as individuals and, by extension, most concerned with personal liberty. We see indications of this in Magna Carta, the English Civil War, Protestantism and the fact that Great Britain was the first major country to abolish slavery, a process starting with the famous case of Somerset versus Stewart in 1772. These are actually highly spiritual matters because individuality is what makes a created being start to become a god in its own right, and the sense of personal liberty is what gives a material being release from the control of matter into the freedom of spirit. This is why the Creator created, to make, to put it somewhat naively, friends and companions as opposed to mindless slaves, fellow creative beings who could contribute to universal life and make it more.

Now, the process can go wrong. If individuality becomes important for its own sake and seeks to serve itself rather than God it has, so to speak, gone bad. But if it aligns itself with the creative purpose of the universe and seeks harmonious interaction with other individuals, it is carrying out God's will and furthering its own spiritual fulfilment.

By this line of thinking it would be no accident that English became a kind of lingua franca in the nineteenth and twentieth centuries and continues to be so. The gift of individuality, hitherto present but relatively undeveloped, spread throughout all the nations of the world. This was a major step forward in human evolution. Now what is needed is for this individual sense of self to connect with the greater Self of the universe. Having become conscious of itself it needs to learn to go beyond itself but it could not do this without first knowing itself. It is the sense of separation that allows for fully conscious union.

'I' is the basic reality in the universe. It is how God would describe himself. I, the one without a second. It is what consciousness reduces to. The eternal subject. God's great gift to his creation was to bestow his supreme sense of self on us human beings so that we could become like him. This is what being made in his image means and it is an idea expressed in English more fully than in any other language. This was the task of the English speaking peoples, to bring to the forefront of consciousness the full sense of what it is to be an individual. Any free son of God must be an individual but individuality is totally opposed to equality so one can see the drive for more and more equality as an attack on individuality and an attempt to return a state of freedom to one of uniformity and conformity. It may seem progressive to those who adopt this cause as a matter of social or political development but the push towards equality must also be seen as profoundly anti-evolutionary.

Why I Am Not a Conservative

I would imagine that many people who might be interested in a book that sets out the case against equality would regard themselves as on the right but I don't think of myself in those terms. I am certainly not on the left and never have been but I don't see myself as a conservative (even with a small 'c') either. There are many things from the past that I would wish to conserve and I do see leftism, used as a general descriptive term, as the main source through which spiritual damage and nihilism have been introduced into the modern world, but that does not mean we should return to a time before this anti-spiritual political philosophy arose. For one thing, the past was very imperfect which is why the spirit of reform was justified, but more significantly, human consciousness evolves and what was right at one time ceases to be right at another.

I recently read a book by the Russian philosopher Nikolai Berdyaev about Dostoyevsky who was my favourite author back in the days when I read fiction. Him and Tolkien anyway, a strange couple you might think but each could be said to fill in the gaps of the other. Berdyaev says of Dostoyevsky that he should

> not be regarded as a conservative or reactionary in the current sense. He was revolutionary-minded in a deeper way. He saw no possibility of a return to the conception of life, a static and immovable form, that existed before the arising of the revolutionary spirit. He was the first to notice how movements gain impetus in the world, the whole tending towards an end. 'The end of the world is coming,' he wrote in his notebook. This is not the attitude of a conservative. His hostility against revolution was not that of a man with a stale mind who takes some interest or other in the old social order, but the hostility of an apocalyptic being who takes the side of Christ in

his supreme struggle with Antichrist. Now he who marches with Christ with his face towards the last great battle at the end of time is a man of the future and not of the past, every bit as much as him who marches with Antichrist. The conflict between revolutionaries and counter-revolutionaries is a superficial affair between the has-beens who have been supplanted and the supplanters who now have the first places at feasts. Dostoyevsky stood aside from that contest and was ranged among those for whom revolution of the spirit opposes the spirit of revolution.

There is more in this vein but the point I wish to make is this. The past has gone. Much that was good has been destroyed but it cannot be restored in the form in which it existed any more than we can bring back the glories of ancient Egypt, the loss of which were so lamented in the Prophecy of Hermes. What we need to do is re-establish the spirit that built the form of the past but find new ways in which to express it. And that spirit will also be different because we are different. Human consciousness has changed. It is more self-aware and that is a necessary development. It is why the past cannot be brought back.

Conservatives favour a return to or preservation of the form of the past. Whilst agreeing that much has been jettisoned that was noble and beautiful, we must make a clear distinction between form and spirit. What really matters is that the connection to spirit is maintained or, in our case, restored. If and when that happens a new form will arise that grows out of the new spiritual awareness but, at the same time, will be built on the same principles as the structures of the past. Materialistic revolutionaries destroy in order to completely remake but spiritual evolutionists seek to fulfil the law and the prophets not to overturn them.

The battle is not between right and left and those that think it is will find themselves in one way or another on the side of the left. The battle is between the forces of Christ and those of the Antichrist, between divine creation and that which attempts to undermine, reframe or destroy divine creation. We have to keep our eyes fixed on the spiritual ball and not be led astray by what are ultimately only worldly things. It's because conservatives often are so led astray, and also because they don't properly appreciate the evolutionary nature of human consciousness and unfoldment, that I am not a conservative.

On the other hand, supposing the matter went to court and I had to answer a charge of being a conservative (still with the small 'c'). Everything depends on definition, after all. I would still maintain that humanity is on a path of spiritual evolution and therefore cannot remain as it was. I would still say that I believe in progress but I believe in spiritual progress which always builds on the past, even though it may introduce new dimensions of being. However, it should be organic meaning it must grow from its roots. Any growth, or imagined or claimed growth, that is not from the roots is a perversion and a deviation. It is a cancer. Our vaunted modern growth, what we call progress, is, for the most part, a cancer. It is a response to stimulation from the higher worlds and that is as it should be, but it is a response from lower being and self-will. The warmth of the sun causes both weeds and beautiful flowers to grow. Modern materialistic civilisation is a powerful and choking weed spreading unchecked that has flourished in the dark heavy manure of sin and is driving out more delicate and sensitive flowers, both ones that were already planted and ones that were waiting to be put in the ground.

If I am a conservative then a conservative such as myself would be one who values the past and is loyal to the best of the past but is not blind to its failings. He sees how the beauty and wisdom of past achievement were sincere responses to divine impulse and attempts to express the truth and glory of God. He also sees how much of humanity's artistic and philosophical productions of the last two centuries have been a response to the devil, celebrating ugliness, sin and perversion with the excuse that these are a natural part of life instead of signs of spiritual failure. He doesn't want to return to the past because he is a modern man with a modern man's awareness of self but he regards it, for the most part and with provisos but certainly in respect of its higher elements, as a genuine attempt to respond to the spiritual life. We are not the people we were and can never be again, nor should we be, but we can certainly recognise that we were going along a path that led, more or less, in the right direction albeit with many twists and turns, came to a fork in the road and took the wrong turning. We should have gone straight ahead but turned left and the path we took is leading downwards.

This is the only sense in which I am a conservative. As someone who recognises that the past for all its faults was frequently an attempt to engage with God, and that tradition sought to preserve that in a fallen world. Whereas, in the present time for all our undoubted material achievements we have succumbed to spiritual corruption and are consequently putting up an increasing number of barriers in our consciousness to goodness, beauty and truth.

I return to Berdyaev's description of Dostoyevsky. The point to take away from this is that the spiritual man stands above any question of politics. There may be elements of political thought to which he responds and these will probably often be drawn from the traditional side because that acknowledged God and saw man's life as centred in the spiritual whereas leftism, despite some early religious grounding, is rooted in this world. It does not see man as descended from heaven but rising up from the earth and that is the cause of its illusions. However, the spiritual man does not think in terms of right and left but of Christ and Antichrist. Everything else is just a distraction and a sideshow.

It is the increased sense of what it is to be an individual with the greater understanding of freedom and the more developed creativity that separates us from the men of the past. This was the new phase of spiritual growth that came about and is why a return to traditional ways of being and thinking that were suitable to earlier forms of consciousness is no longer viable. And yet that does not mean we should do as we have done and reject them more or less wholesale. Adapt and adjust would have been a more enlightened path to have taken. Conservatives are right to seek to protect tradition but mistaken when they ignore the need for change and development. However, for this change to be genuine progress it must respect the wisdom of the past. If it denies the spiritual wisdom of the ages and tries to rebuild the world on entirely new foundations, as we are doing, the building will collapse. We in the twenty-first century are sons and daughters of the Revolution and, for all its political posturing, the Revolution was a revolution against God.

Tolerance and Humanism

Here is another casualty of the push towards ever more equality. Tolerance from being a virtue now teeters on the edge of becoming a vice. For if everything and everyone is equal then all manner of behaviour must be accepted. Eventually nothing is wrong. Good and evil themselves become just two different approaches, neither one actually better than the other. We haven't reached that stage yet and it is unlikely we ever really could but the borders between the two can be blurred and that does happen today, particularly with regard to sexual morality where increasingly it's all just a matter of taste while the order of creation, built into the universe from the beginning, is disregarded.

I would not be writing this in a world in which people really did condemn others who were just not the same as themselves but in today's world tolerance does not mean that. When you allow all sorts of aberrant behaviour and equate the sinful with the virtuous or the unnatural with the natural, tolerance has descended into lack of discrimination and lowered standards. Then it is a sign not of a humane society but a corrupted one in which culture and civilisation are declining from an enlightened state to a barbarous one. This is where we are now.

There is no true civilisation which is not based on an awareness of the spiritual. This may be expressed in different ways but in all of them the transcendent is regarded as an absolute good and the model on which life on Earth should be patterned. There is a recognition that we are natural beings but also spiritual ones and the natural, without being denied, should always conform to the spiritual. This necessarily creates hierarchy and all true civilisations are indeed hierarchical though with the proviso that all parts of the hierarchy are respected and the higher exists to serve the whole not itself. An analogy with the human body is frequently used.

So much trouble comes from the misuse of words and of not defining them correctly. Tolerance can mean putting up with something that you feel to be annoying or it can mean allowing something that is objectively wrong, but these are two quite different things. Annoying is just a personal matter. Wrong is universal. I can be tolerant of a baby crying in my train carriage but not tolerant of someone hitting the baby. Even liberals would acknowledge that but when it comes to behaviour that conflicts with the pattern of heaven, they are not so observant. This is because they do not acknowledge a pattern of heaven but then that is a deficiency within themselves. It's not because, as they might claim, religious belief is a personal matter that should not be imposed on others. Every society imposes beliefs of some sort. Modern liberals certainly do or try to do so. But an awareness of the spiritual is within each human soul unless that awareness is crushed by the outer world and the ideologies it might impose on the soul. However, even then the soul has its own freedom and a soul true to its inner nature should still acknowledge the reality and supremacy of the spiritual. God exists within each one of us. We may choose not to acknowledge this because he doesn't force himself, but he is there.

Any single virtue if emphasised to the exclusion of other virtues becomes a vice. If it is given disproportionate attention, it tips over from being a good to a bad thing. This is easy to see when courage becomes foolhardiness or prudence cowardice. Chastity can become cold sterility, patience can become inertia, kindness weakness and so on. In our day tolerance has become an excuse for laxness and the disregard of spiritual truth to pander to human feelings. This is a sure indication of a corrupt society, one that seeks pleasure and tries to avoid pain of any sort. Earthly pain is always regarded as an evil instead of being a sign that we are in this world to learn to overcome our attachments to the lower self and its desires.

It is often instructive to seek out the root meaning of words. Tolerance comes from a Latin word meaning to endure, specifically pain or hardship. Hence it means to put up with without complaint. But to go from that to accepting what is wrong in the name of an all things are equally valid ideology or believing that the existence of something is its own justification is a complete deformation of meaning. This is an excellent example of how, when you remove the over-arching yardstick of a spiritual absolute, you are left with the consequence that nothing means anything.

Tolerance today is an aspect of humanism which is the basic belief system of the modern era. The problem is that humanism in its current form is fundamentally anti-human because, despite its avowed aim of ennobling man, it actually degrades him as it denies that in him which raises him beyond the natural world. Its rejection of God takes away our status as a spiritual being come to Earth and at a stroke abolishes the sense of higher and lower (closer to God or further away from him), reducing the human soul to a mere by-product of material forces. Then, with its goal of seeking to eradicate suffering, humanism isolates man in this world, banishing him from his true home in the spiritual realm. This is because the reality of tragedy in this life which so offends the humanist comes from the fact that we are part animal and part angel. It is the conflict between these two aspects of our being that is responsible for suffering at a level beyond the purely physical. If you get rid of tragedy, you get rid of the spiritual. It is obviously not wrong to address the fact of suffering but to seek to remove the possibility of it altogether as seems to be the humanist end goal would be to kill the human soul. This is not meant as an excuse to ignore suffering but an attempt to show the inner cause and even, up to a point, spiritual necessity of it. Suffering is mysteriously tied up with love. If you remove the possibility of the one you also remove the possibility of the other. Indeed, it may well be that we only love in a spiritual sense to the degree that we either have suffered or are able to suffer. I have often noticed that the faces of the people I regard as the most spiritually aware are those that have suffering etched into them. Suffering gives depth, not inevitably but it can do depending on how one reacts to it. This is a truth the materialistic humanist ignores and one demonstrated by Christ.

When Man tries to become more than Man by himself, he becomes less than Man. Without the idea that he is a son of God, in his deepest nature a being not of this world, he can never go beyond himself. And yet the essence of true humanity is that we can go beyond our earthly selves. That reality lies behind all our greatest achievements and best ideas of ourselves and our place in the universe. However, if we are to go beyond ourselves we cannot do that as ourselves as we experience ourselves to be now. We have to see ourselves as spiritual beings not earthly ones. The great mistake of many religious people is to think that they can take their earthly self, their normal human self, intact to heaven. Not so. All spiritual teachers who know what they are talking about have proclaimed that it is not change but transformation we need. In the humanist conception of man transformation is impossible because the human being is a material being only. Matter cannot change into spirit unless spirit is already present as the underlying reality.

Humanism has led to the smashing of the hierarchy of good. We no longer recognise the higher as higher or the lower as lower because we no longer recognise God as God and what the reality of God actually means. Without God as the highest reality the ladder of being is levelled to the ground and qualitative differences are negated. Humanism, which ostensibly sought to raise man, has only succeeded in dragging him down. Looking at the present situation in the world, that process is still taking place. We are being dragged further down. If man does not know himself to be potentially a god, does he then become just another beast? Or does he sink lower than that? At least a beast is true to its own nature.

Some humanists think we will evolve to a higher state of consciousness but fail to understand that evolution in this sense only brings out what is already there. It doesn't come from nothing as the higher cannot come from the lower. Even more foolish, indeed inhuman, are the transhumanists who imagine that by melding man and machine they can create a higher being. If they ever succeed in this unholy operation, they will find they have only created a living hell.

Human beings have tried innumerable ways to reach heaven without acknowledging the reality of God and Christ because they have not been willing to make the sacrifice this entails. But it is a good sacrifice that only requires the giving up of our spiritual sickness. The unrepentant ego is like a cancer and it must be cut out. There is some pain in this but the alternative is death. Humanism is the path that leads to death. Yes, man is a noble creature with unlimited potential but only when he takes his place as a son of God. Without God man is nothing but a vainglorious braggart swollen with self-importance but inwardly empty.

All proposed answers to the questions posed by life in this world must include a moral response. For humanism the moral philosophy is summed up by the golden rule of do as you would be done by. This ties in with our concern for egalitarianism and our insistence on tolerance. It is the driving force behind them. Now obviously this is not a bad philosophy but, as it stands, it is a limited one. We cannot know the right way to act even to ourselves never mind our neighbours if we do not know what a human being is or what is the goal towards which we should be moving.

The humanist does not believe in God but he does believe in this abstraction of humanity. Setting aside whether there is such a thing as humanity or whether there are just human beings, I

117

would point out that humanity without a divine maker who has given it its own spiritual life and freedom is nothing more than an assemblage of atoms driven by mechanical forces. To talk of love or goodness in these terms is ludicrous. You are not real and neither am I. There is no centre to your being and you cannot in any meaningful way actually matter. You are nothing. Human beings only have any kind of integrity to their being if they have spiritual integrity. Without God we are empty vessels with no authentic individuality.

What humanism does is borrow or steal ideas which can only have any substance in a spiritual universe and apply them to itself. This cannot work because what gives these ideas reality in the first place is being denied. It is like trying to climb while denying the fact of height. Individuality, freedom, love have no meaning in a purely material universe and to pretend otherwise is blatant self-deception.

This matters. You cannot say that as long as we accept individuality, freedom and love, it doesn't matter if we don't acknowledge where they come from. If you don't acknowledge their source, you put yourself at opposition with the things themselves which become shadows of their true selves. You are living in a world of fakes and make-believe. You are an imposter, a thief. If individuality, freedom and love only exist because of God then to construct a world and a philosophy and a mode of being that denies God but tries to retain these things is to live a lie. A denier of God has no reason to care for anything because there is nothing except himself and neither he nor anyone else is real in any meaningful sense, never mind the fact that neither he nor anyone else will last long anyway.

The bottom line is that the humanist has replaced God with self which means that self is eventually promoted to God. This is why a man today can become a woman or thinks he can. I make my own reality. I am God. There is no absolute truth. I can be what I want to be.

When the real Christ is abandoned, a false Christ arises, in the realm of ideas at first but possibly, as we discussed earlier, even in reality later on. This false Christ will appear as a humanitarian. He will preach tolerance to all, universal equality, the brotherhood of man. But his humanitarianism will be an end in itself not part of an over-riding approach to God. He may talk of God but his God will have to fit into the general materialistic attitude with our life in this world seen as primary. He will talk of progress, improvement, development but all these things relate to making the same thing better or apparently better. The spiritual path is not about improvement but transcendence. It does not look to make better men but new men who may be formed from the old men but are more properly described as transformed. Humanism keeps us in spiritual darkness because it can never liberate us from the merely human.

The Lowest of the Low

An argument for equality from a spiritual point of view might be that in a monastery, which is supposed to be where the religious life is lived to the full, all monks are regarded as equal. But before jumping to any conclusions we need to examine this more closely. Setting aside the point that there are still abbots and novices in a monastery, and that a spiritual hierarchy certainly does exist even if a more worldly one of privilege does not, a factor to consider is that a monastery is not actually an example of a spiritual environment. It is rather an environment in which souls are being trained to be spiritual which is a different matter. A monastery is, in a sense, an artificial world in which the ordinary natural life is set aside for a higher purpose. Hence, it cannot be taken as a prototype for an ideal society. The fact that all monasteries are single sex institutions should also alert us to that. Monasteries have an important, at times vital, part to play in evolving human consciousness. Even if you disregard their spiritual function, they have preserved art and culture at times when these were in danger of being lost in the outside world, the European Dark Ages being a case in point. But they must still be seen as unnatural environments and they do not provide a template for how we should be living nor are they illustrative of a higher state of being. There will be no monasteries in heaven. There will be no need for them.

When I was being instructed by the Masters, I was told that '**in order to cultivate humility you should think of yourself as the lowest of the low**.' I don't believe I was being told I actually was the lowest of the low but I was being given a spiritual exercise to perform. It was similar to the *upaya* of Mahayana Buddhism which is translated as 'skilful means', and is something that may not be literally true but which is expedient in that it may work on the mind to bring about a desired result. Basically, it is a practical device, even a technique, that will help a disciple get to a stage he might not be able to attain so well otherwise.

Spiritual training employs various methods to bring the soul closer to where it ought to be. It puts the disciple in situations he must negotiate his way through with the aim that he may be altered during the journey. The chief lesson on the spiritual path is to overcome the ego and to achieve this the student may be subjected to a variety of tests and even apparent humiliations during his training. This is not done to belittle him but to enable him to rise above self-will, egotistical reactions and pride. He may be required to experience situations in which he must deal with other people on the basis of equality or even in an inferior position because he must learn that all men are the children of God and that he is not more important because of his greater spiritual awareness. The reality may be that he actually is more spiritually aware, presumably that is so or he would not be in that situation of training, but he must not feel it of himself. He must understand that, in the words of the Masters, 'an evolved person should never feel superior to anyone else on account of his evolution. The Master Jesus and all the Masters of old had preached humility and demonstrated it too. They knew that they were as nothing and that all they were came from the Creator. Without humility you can reach a certain point on the path but then, if you do not acquire it, you will go no further.'

Jesus did not behave to his disciples as though he was a superior person. By washing their feet in public he even reversed the customary hierarchy as it would have been expressed outwardly. And yet he clearly knew he was superior for there wouldn't have been much point in him teaching if that weren't the case. The disciples also acknowledged this. The simple truth is that every soul is made in the image of God and every soul is due respect on that account. At the same time, none are equal as such. Even among the disciples there were those, Peter, James and John being obvious examples, who were closer to the

Master and more privileged than others. To learn humility you may sometimes need to see yourself as the lowest of the low as a disciplinary corrective to normal human egotism, but this is a training tool. Great souls are aware of their station but they also know that everything comes from God so their attainments, spiritual or otherwise, are not their own but his.

*

Those who have read my earlier book *Meeting the Masters* will be familiar with the idea of spiritual beings who are, according to different descriptive terms, liberated, enlightened, one with God, spiritually realised or members of the Kingdom of Heaven. These are human souls who have learned the lessons of this world and graduated into full membership of the spiritual realm. They have overcome the world, the flesh and the devil both outwardly and within themselves, and as a result have entered the life more abundant. When they spoke to me, I certainly did not feel I was their equal. They never talked down to me or made me feel I was their inferior but their spiritual pre-eminence was obvious. I knew it and they knew it. It was just a fact but it sat alongside the other fact of love. Every time they spoke to me they talked of love and they demonstrated it too. It was the ever-present undercurrent to everything they did.

It's worth thinking about love from the equality perspective because religious people need to recapture the idea of love from secular humanists who have taken it over and recast it according to their limited conception of what a human being is. We all feel love. It seems that even some animals, dogs in particular, are capable of love of a sort. Love is a basic reality of conscious existence, specifically of self-conscious existence, but there are aspects of love and we should be aware of it in its spiritual form which is the root and source of all other forms.

When Christ came to this world his principal message was one of love. Love God and love your neighbour as yourself are the two great commandments, but what was this love of which he spoke? Nowadays we tend to understand spiritual love in terms of empathy or compassion but I believe this is a mistake. Divine love is fully personal and directed like a powerful beam of light whereas empathy and compassion have a diffused all things to all men quality to them. They are a warm blanket as opposed to a passionate intensity. The moon, shining by reflected light, as opposed to the sun blazing away with its own fire. They are kind but they do not cast out fear or lay down their lives for their friends. To forestall objections that on occasion they might have done just that, I would ask you to distinguish between being inspired by genuine love and being motivated by a kind of compassion ideology. There is even in some people a pathology of compassion that arises when a person falls victim to the glamour of love and of being the one who loves, and who therefore loves as a self-conscious act. Such a person might not be aware of this so it is not simply a pose but nor is it a response of spontaneous, unaffected, heartfelt love.

Divine love or humanitarian compassion? Which do we choose? One important difference between the two lies in full acceptance of freedom and suffering for the sake of spiritual good. Those who respond to divine love see man's destiny in God and will accept anything to follow that path. By contrast, the merely compassionate look for happiness and well-being in this world. Do we seek our end in this life or in the higher life in God? Do we seek freedom and responsibility in terms of divine being and creation or is it just the removal of suffering that motivates us and determines our feelings?

The first commandment is to love God. This points to the fact, not appreciated by humanitarians, that real love is only possible in God. Only when you love God who is the source of love can you begin to know love as it really is and not just as it is reflected in the mortal human heart. We are back to the moon and the sun. Divine love cannot be known by those who do not love God, and the more we respond to divine love the more will that love affect all other loves which only exist because of God's love. Humanitarian compassion is obviously a good thing in its own way, but it is chiefly for those who do not yet understand the love of God and make do with a lesser substitute that only operates on the material level.

The Masters spoke of themselves as one, members of a heavenly body, and they were in that sense equals. But it was not the whole story. They also spoke of higher Masters, great souls who had progressed to even more elevated states of being. On a few occasions I was spoken to by these Masters. Those who think in terms of the expansions of consciousness known as initiations might see this as examples of beings who have gone on to greater initiations and penetrated more deeply into the mind of God. Their existence tells us that spiritual evolution does not cease when a soul has transcended identification with the material world but carries on, I am tempted to say, forever. On the rare occasions the higher Masters did speak to me it was as though they were communicating from a deep and distant dimension of being far from this earthly condition yet encompassing it totally with their love and wisdom. One actually described himself as coming from a far-off place and spoke of 'the mysteries of your cosmic law' giving the impression that the problems and limitations of human consciousness were a long way off from his current state of being but he was still in total sympathy with souls struggling in this world. They conveyed a sense of profound peace, truly the peace that passes all understanding which is very different to mere absence of disturbance. They encouraged me to acquire this inner peace in words which I will quote directly as they are most pertinent to our present time when the spiritual has been chased from the world and evil is all about us, often the worse for not being recognised as such.

'Do not let yourself be disturbed by anything that happens outwardly. What takes place outwardly is not your responsibility but what happens within is. No matter how wrong you think something is, no matter how contrary to the good and the true you consider it, you should not react to it inwardly. Perfect love at all times is the way of the Masters and you should follow that way too.'

I wish I could say I had learned this lesson which is similar to Jesus' instruction not to resist evil. It does not mean we should turn a blind eye to evil or let evil get its way without fighting it. It is saying we should not be affected within by evil, not let it provoke hatred or anger. Evil must be fought but you should not allow it, or any aspect of it, to gain a foothold in your heart. This involves trusting God. Today, when we witness the spread of evil, that can be a challenge but this is one of the lessons for all disciples at the present time. This is the test to which we are being subjected because now the call is not just for people who believe in God but people who can act as little outposts of God in a world that has fallen into darkness. In a very real sense, every believer today is called to become a saint.

There is a parallel to the idea of Masters and higher Masters who all serve in the same spiritual hierarchy but at different levels. It is that of angels and archangels. All angels serve God as his messengers and agents, fulfilling many and varied functions in the creation, and their tasks differ according to rank. In Christianity they are arranged in different orders or 'choirs' with the most common scheme, that of Pseudo-Dionysius detailed in his work *On the Celestial Hierarchy*, stretching through nine levels from ordinary angels to cherubim and seraphim. We recognise guardian angels who are assigned to every soul as a behind the scenes guide through earthly life but there are also angels associated with the form building side of life, with the elements, with the natural world in all its varied states and even with the nations. They are God's messengers and helpers and are to be found on all levels of being from Earth rising right up to the Throne of God. They are specifically spoken of as a hierarchy. There is no equality even among the angels.

The Most High

On several occasions the Masters spoke to me of the Most High. This is a term of biblical origin and a translation of the Hebrew word *Elyon* or *El Elyon* which first appears in the Book of Genesis chapter 14 verse 18 where Melchizedek King of Salem is described as a priest of the Most High. In the following verse Melchizedek blesses the patriarch Abram (Abraham to be) saying 'Blessed be Abram by God Most High, Creator of Heaven and Earth'. The term is also used by Moses in Deuteronomy chapter 32 when he speaks of the Most High dividing the nations, and it further occurs in Isaiah and the Psalms, always referring to the Supreme Being.

The Masters would sometimes pass on greetings and blessings from the Most High, and they told me that what they taught came from the Most High. They did not define this term but left it to me to understand intuitively. That was their method. They sought to awaken the mind in the heart not to convey information one could look up in a book. It was my responsibility to ask a question if I sought deeper understanding, but I realised they were not there to satisfy my curiosity. The purpose of their visits was to train me spiritually and their time was not to be wasted. They used words and phrases to trigger responses and I believe their use of this particular phrase was to suggest something of the nature of God. It has a resonance that takes it beyond a simple superlative to a descriptive term that impresses the mind with the power and majesty of divine being and the transcendent glory of God.

God is the Most High. This means he stands above creation as its progenitor. Above Earth but also above Heaven as he is the Creator of both – see the words of Melchizedek. He is the peak of existence beyond which there is nothing. No one shares this place with God. As the Most High he is alone and all one. His abode is the transcendent dimension of pure being and as pure being God has no form. He simply is. This is the world of eternity. Early religions associated the Creator God with the sky as this was the highest region they knew. Always there has been this idea that God was the Most High, greater height being regarded as synonymous with greater reality, greater meaning, greater truth. Even now we cannot avoid the correlation of height and greater consciousness. We talk of higher consciousness, higher planes, higher reality. The Most High is still the place we locate God.

Creation can be understood as God expressing himself. We may envisage this as the highest plane of spirit projecting itself downwards into matter where the one becomes many and the formless takes on a multitude of different forms, rejoicing in the diverse aspects of manifested life. Or else we can look at the process as a single central point radiating outwards in self-expression through all the numberless worlds and forms of being. For the Hindus this is God's *lila* or play which is a beautiful way of expressing things but perhaps we might also think of it as God almost showing off. 'Look' he exclaims triumphantly, 'This is what I can do! This is what I am capable of!'. In Islam it is said that God was a hidden treasure and wanted to reveal himself. That idea also seems to capture something of the truth.

At the unmanifested level of the Most High before creation takes place there is perfect oneness. Creation is a break in oneness and the first break is the one becoming two. When, to initiate his creative activity, God says 'Let there be light' he divides himself into the Creator and the substance out of which creation is fashioned which is light. There is a parallel with Eve being taken out of the sleeping Adam who represents the unmanifested state. From this primeval light are formed all the worlds so in this scenario God the Creator is the Father and the light which gives form to manifested existence is the Mother. These are the active and passive modes of being; it is the interaction between the two that gives rise to phenomenal existence.

God forms the higher levels of the universe out of light and thus begins the process of creation. From this foundation there develops a hierarchical substructure of levels of being which are the many planes of conscious existence ranging from highest spirit down to the material world in which we live. All these can be imagined as the garments of God, the Creator clothing his spiritual energy in form, and each plane is inhabited by a variety of spiritual beings who possess individual self-consciousness as well as the ability to co-create (at their level) with God. Thus, the universe is a shared project between God and his creation who, being created in his image, can join him in forming a universe of ever more beauty and varied expression.

The hierarchical structure of the universe with spheres of consciousness ranging from the most high level down to the physical world with spiritual beings existing on every rung of the ladder is a direct riposte to the concept of equality. This whole structure and all the beings are ultimately one in God but within that oneness there are vast differences in awareness and expression though all are evolving towards greater awareness and expression unless they take the step of rejecting God and thereby moving out of the process of unfolding more and more of their divine potential. Life is expressed in an innumerable diversity of form, and diversity means inequality. All are God's children and all are loved but all are not equal in the eyes of the Most High. What matters is not that the different expressions of life should be equal one to another but that they should seek to become more like God, who is the Father of them all, in the context of their own intrinsic form and nature.

God is the Most High. The phrase refers to a being and to the source of being. It is both the apex of creation and that which exists beyond creation. It is the point at which spiritual life pours into the universe and also where the garments of God, the various spheres of manifested being, have been shed and divine reality stands revealed in its naked splendour. Our spiritual preceptors are consciously in touch with this level and seek to bring us up to it so that we too may know God according to our own capacity for such knowledge. Even in terms of union with God there is the personal element. The saints are one with God and each other but they are not equal.

Death, the Great Equaliser?

We all die and return to the dust from whence we arose. Are we then all equal in death? From the material point of view this must be the case. We have come from the equality of non-existence and return to that state in which everything is reduced to nothing, the perfect state of equality. But from the spiritual point of view our inequality becomes more pronounced. In the spiritual world we are judged after death and go to wherever that judgement determines; that is, our consciousness becomes focused in the environment that reflects it. The word judged means assessed and is a purely objective affair. There is no jury because there is no uncertainty. We are judged completely dispassionately according to what we are, our spiritual quality or lack of it, what we have done or not done, believed or not believed, taking belief as foundational to being and not merely intellectual. We are examined on an individual basis and receive according to our inner condition which will be unique in every case. Death from the spiritual perspective is the least equal thing there can be. It happens to everyone, high and low, so is equalising in that respect but what happens after death differs greatly depending on who and what we are. Certainly, worldly inequalities will count for nothing but spiritual ones will be determining.

All religious people need to have at least some understanding of death and what it is. In truth, everyone needs this since we all die but those who are serious about the spiritual life should do so in particular. We can start simply by saying that death is the shedding of the physical body and the release of the soul into the spiritual world, but then we have to ask what is the soul and what is the spiritual world?

In the post-mortem sense the soul is you, your mind and character which, to begin with at least, remain unchanged.

The body is gone and one must assume that all conditions, mental as well as physical, that were linked to the body and the brain are removed. Does this mean that the blind can see and the senile regain their faculties? I would doubt there is a sudden and dramatic change as that might be too shocking but there may be a gradual lifting of the darkness, both visual and psychological. Then the person stands forth as he is. But where is he? That depends on the person. In the spiritual world outer reflects inner so your environment after death will reflect your spiritual state. For some that might mean a plane of dimness and emptiness. A confirmed atheist may even remain unconscious for a while if he has convinced himself that death is the end. For others there will be light in the double sense of illumination and the feeling of no longer being pulled down and trapped by the heaviness of matter. A positive attitude towards death is extremely important as that will liberate you from some of the ancient fears and restrictions that surround it and have such a debilitating psychological effect. If you can approach death in a spirit of optimism, which doesn't preclude an inevitable apprehension for you are, after all, entering on a great mystery, that will be most beneficial to your further progress.

For everyone the death of the physical body will sooner or later be followed by the stripping of self. The physical body has been shed but there remain layers of falseness and artificiality that we have built up and surrounded ourselves with as a shield and defence and wall against life while in the world. We all have an image of ourself with which we identify and which we project outwards and this must be dismantled completely before we are ready to move on to more celestial regions.

Thus, the first thing to be done after death if we wish to ascend and not remain as though becalmed on lower levels of consciousness is purification. This corresponds to purgatory in the Christian tradition. Only the pure can enter a world of purity. There can be no darkness in heaven. However, this will not apply to everyone in the same way for while some do at least aspire to progress spiritually, others do not. There will be worlds corresponding to hell in which the soul suffers the consequences of its attachment to one or several of the various sins, and others more like limbo where the great mass of souls probably find themselves. Limbo is a kind of semi-material world that interpenetrates the physical and is like the astral plane or desire world of occultism. The astral plane itself has many levels, some of which may be dark and dull, others reflecting higher forms of consciousness but these are all the creation of the created which is to say the outgrowth of human desire, imagination and thought. In these worlds the soul when it has found its appropriate place will be happy with all earthly woes and problems removed. It can live as it likes but it will not know God or the higher spiritual realities though there may be an imitation of these to which the conventionally religious may gravitate, and here they stay until they experience the inner urge to move on and progress to higher levels. Some may even think they are in heaven for this is a state of natural happiness in which the earthly kinds of desires can be satisfied. But there is no real spiritual fulfilment and no consciousness of the presence of God. The conventionally good person may gravitate here as well as those who are still attached to the phenomenal side of life.

At higher levels we may find regions corresponding to the prelapsarian Paradise, and also to the heavens of the various pagan religions. The spiritual law is like attracts like so what you are is where you go. To get to higher/subtler realms you must work to eradicate that in you which acts as ballast, essentially sin and ignorance, and encourage the finer feelings of spiritual aspiration and attraction to what is noble and good. Part of this involves developing imagination but not in the worldly sense in which we understand that word now. True imagination is receptivity to higher things. It is linked to spiritual sensitivity.

Paradise is spiritual but it is not divine, the difference being that it is still part of Creation. Above Paradise there is the true Heaven which is where the fully purified soul stands in the presence of the Creator who is now known as the very essence of your own soul. He is still God the Creator but he is also fully immanent. There is no separation between you and him. However, Heaven is not a single place where every soul is the same as every other soul. If anything, souls in heaven are more individual not less so and more individual means less equal. They are now fully themselves, a unique aspect of God, now completed, but at the same time while every soul in heaven may be filled with God, there is always more God to be known and so every soul stands at a point in which God may be at the centre of their being but they can always move closer to the centre of God's being. Likewise, they can expand the circumference of their conscious being. The law of life is growth and this continues in Heaven as it must or else Heaven would have a lack in it. It is not pure being as opposed to becoming but being and becoming together, always working to create something more.

Here I must introduce the vexed question of reincarnation. As a believer in that mechanism for the education of souls I would say that most souls, after a spell in one or several of the inner planes, experience an urge to return to Earth to further their development in a sphere in which that is possible, the material plane of full separation. Those who ascend to Heaven after life in this world are probably fewer in number than we have been told. At either end of the human spectrum there are those who are damned and those who are fully saved but many souls, in my opinion, need to return and continue with their course of spiritual development in this world.

I will add a proviso. This might have been the pattern of the past but we are at the conclusion of an age. Now, souls may be facing an end of term examination in which their future paths are determined. It may be that the course is ending and souls must make definitive choices. That is my personal feeling. It also explains the vastly expanded world population. We are being called either to go up higher or, if we refuse to embrace that destiny, to fall back. The tests are coming thick and fast and it may well be that *wide is the gate, and broad is the way, that leadeth to destruction, and many there be which go in thereat: (but) strait is the gate, and narrow is the way, which leadeth unto life, and few there be that find it* (Matthew 7:13–14). Words to take seriously now more than ever when everything in the world is conspiring to lead us to the wide gate and broad way. The day of our death may be the single most important day of our life because it is its culminating point and the moment at which we give our conclusive answer to the question that has been asked of us throughout our life. God sends us away from himself to see how we will behave when the spiritual cord is cut. Life is many things but one of the most important is an examination of the heart. At death you must hand in your paper for marking. You don't have to get a perfect score or anything like but you should at least have tried to answer the questions asked as well as you can.

Good and Evil, Spirit and Matter, Creator and Creation

I imagine that even the most enthusiastic supporter of the equality doctrine would stop short of claiming that good and evil were equal. But why if nothing is better than anything else and anything that exists in the world is as justified as anything else that exists? It's true that no one in the public eye has officially gone this far yet but if we proceed on our current path of value inversion and post-modern deconstruction of concepts of right and wrong, it's not hard to predict that there will eventually be someone who puts forward the idea. At first it will be entertained by only a few pioneers in new thought as they will probably consider themselves, the temptation to be part of the elite being one of the strongest temptations there is. But then it will drip through to the mainstream as these things do. It is unlikely to be framed in such a bald way as I have just put it but the implications will be there, and the effects of blurring the boundaries between traditional ideas of good and evil will manifest themselves as a consequence of the intellectual seeds sown.

In actual fact, there have long been those who believe that the serpent's temptation to Eve in the Garden of Eden was a good thing which bestowed evolutionary benefits by awakening self-consciousness. He was simply doing his job and serving the demands of life in a particular way. This is in line with a certain strain in esoteric thought which considers evil to be necessary for the greater good to come about. It is a kind of resistance required for good to arise by virtue of being forced to push back against it. According to this understanding, evil is simply the darkness against which one can more clearly see the light. If good and evil are not exactly equal in this scheme of things, the lines between them are not so clear cut as traditionally understood. They are two sides of the same coin, and God as the Absolute is beyond good and evil as we think of them in our limited earthly way.

The idea may be intellectually attractive but it is mistaken. Evil is evil. That does not mean that God being God cannot make good come out of evil but that does not justify it in the first place. It remains a wrong and a result of the fallen ego. Lucifer is not Christ's dark twin in some mysterious fashion working with him for long-term evolutionary development. He is not there to enable self-consciousness to arise and grow. He is not a misunderstood good guy. He is a rebel against God not a partner with him. And as a rebel he is not a freedom fighter resisting an oppressive tyrant but a corrupted egotist motivated by resentment and pride. It's important not to get sucked into the glamour of this false idea. Sin does not have to be experienced in order to overcome it. Darkness does not have to be integrated in order for a person to be in some sense whole. Evil is not part of good. Judas was not Christ's true disciple doing his work as a form of self-sacrifice. These are all deceptions and have no part in proper spiritual understanding. To believe that evil is anything other than evil will corrupt the soul. It is like peering into the abyss. Do that and you risk being drawn in.

In an earlier chapter we alluded to the spiritual philosopher Rudolf Steiner. I'm not a Steiner expert but it seems he thought that Lucifer was not really evil *per se* but a kind of evolutionary force that could go wrong yet was fundamentally positive. Some of the Gnostics also thought like this and there are occultists who would agree. I see this as an error of those who either fall prey to the glamour of the esoteric or else over-intellectualise spirituality, forgetting Jesus' words to *Suffer little children for of such is the kingdom of heaven* (Matthew 19:14). This is not telling us not to think but not to over-think. It is echoed in the Masters' words that '**Spiritual truth is simple, but it is easy to get lost in philosophical speculations which lead nowhere**'. The idea that evil is somehow from a higher perspective good or constructive is one of those deceptive half-truths that can mislead people who think themselves more sophisticated than they are. God can use evil and turn it to good but it remains evil. One should note that Jesus also said (in Matthew 18:7), *Woe to the world because of offenses! For offenses must come, but woe to that man by whom the offense comes!*

If equality really were a metaphysical principle, then even if we did not expect good and evil, which are moral values, to be equal, we might still say that spirit and matter were equal. They are certainly complementary as we have stated when discussing the process of creation, but equal? That is a different thing. Some present-day pagans who believe they are returning to deeper truths that prevailed before the authoritarian and intolerant Christian religion came along but who are really just raking over the coals of atavistic, outmoded spiritualities that pertained to earlier forms of consciousness, blur the boundaries between the spiritual, the psychic and the material in the name of an 'it's all one' philosophy. This is another example of egalitarian thinking. The Goddess Nature is equal to God the Creator as his Consort, they say. She may be that but she is still his creation. Sexuality is just an aspect of spirituality, they say. It may be so but the former must always be seen in the light of the latter which puts it in a very different perspective to how it is normally perceived. Then they suggest that the fallen angels remain angels or gods, they just operate in the vastness of divine reality according to a different agenda to Christian orthodoxy. And so on. While not denying that official Christian religion can be legalistic and unimaginative, and that much is rejected as diabolical that merely does not fit into their narrative (my own experience with the Masters for one), and accepting that Christianity did tend to undervalue the creation and divine immanence, the fact is that proper spirituality has to do with forging a relationship with the Creator. In that relationship, God and the soul are not equal just as the Creator and the creation are not equal and spirit and matter are not equal. In all cases there is a higher and a lower, and while the lower is important, it is still the lower. Matter is the garment of spirit, the aspect of life in which life expresses itself. The true spiritual disciple seeks God and is not distracted by any divine forms that exist within the creation, whether that be the material or spiritual creation. He works from inside out.

*

We have mentioned paganism and it has a bearing on our theme. Modern versions of this ancient creed or groups of creeds could be viewed as reducing spiritual hierarchy to egalitarianism. This is principally with respect to its veneration of the natural world which includes, please note, the psychic levels of material existence and the beings to be found there. Paganism today is not the philosophy of Plato or Plotinus. It is a religion of Nature. That is why it grants such a high place to the Goddess who is none other than the personification of Nature. I do not say that such a being does not, in some form, exist and is not worthy of veneration. I think she does and she is. However, I would maintain that she is part of the created world which means that she can be venerated but not worshipped. Look at the picture on page 41 to get an understanding of the relationship of the Goddess to the Creator. Pagans worship or seek to propitiate the powers of nature and the beings of the inner worlds. Now, there are many powers in the universe, most, though not all, benign. But they are created beings not the Creator and a spiritual path that downplays this reality is not on the same level as one that places it front and centre. That does not mean that a pagan may not be a more spiritually aware person than a Christian but, just as the more enlightened druids accepted Christ as a higher revelation of the divine than that they currently knew, so the truths enshrined in the Christian religion are of a higher order than those to be found in paganism. I would say that paganism can supplement Christianity but should not replace it as it belongs to an earlier world and lacks the higher revelation of the nature of God given by Christ.

Any authentic spiritual practice followed in sincerity and humility will bear good fruit but a paganism which concerns itself with the energies of nature and the earth is not on the same spiritual level as Christianity. The sphere of God is qualitatively superior to that of the gods, and the inner planes of creation remain external to the transcendent Creator.

Paganism was a justifiable spiritual approach in its day but was superseded by the advent of Christ. The pagan deities may at one time have been the transmitters of the divine impulse but when that impulse was withdrawn from them, which it was well over two thousand years ago, something was left which was the vehicles that had embodied that impulse on the psychic level. For when spirit ceases to animate a form it has at one time operated through, that form still remains in the inner worlds though it will start to decay in just the same way as the physical form does when the soul has departed. There is this difference though. The pool of psychic energy left behind by an ancient religion may linger for a long time and can even be given an additional lease of life if attention is directed to it, for example, by ritual or prayer. This does not mean it retains its spiritual virtue as God has withdrawn his gaze from it but it can give the impression of that to those who mistake psychic for spiritual light.

As a matter of fact, it would be my contention that the exact same thing that happened to the ancient pagan religions has happened to Christianity. The animating spirit has started to withdraw from all contemporary religions and that is why they do not satisfy as they used to, and why many people look elsewhere for their spiritual sustenance. However, to seek to revive past approaches to the divine is not the answer as all you will reanimate is the psychic element of the religion. You may also be giving energy to beings on the psychic level who may present themselves as the old gods but who, even if they are in some sense affiliated to past spiritual practices, no longer have a connection to the transcendent realm. The spirit has withdrawn and it will not be going back into old bottles. It never does.

The fact is not all spiritual paths are equal in the sense of being of equal vision and depth. No doubt all paths that have the worship of God at their heart can lead you upwards if followed in sincerity but some are purer channels to truth than others. And while some forms of religion have as their primary purpose to enable us to live in harmony with nature and help attune us to the higher worlds, others have the greater purpose of bringing about the transcending of ego and the union with God. I don't believe that paganism can do this because that is not its real purpose. It is to help us live in the world rather than go beyond it. At the same time, Christianity, like the other monotheistic religions, has the defects of its qualities and undervalues both nature and the body. That leaves a gap which the pagan religions can fill. But they, in their turn, are limited by their emphasis on what the monotheistic religions tend to ignore or downplay which is the Goddess principle. The Goddess is the Mother and specifically Mother Nature but you must go beyond Nature or form, in all its aspects, to find the source of your being which is in spirit or the Father.

The advent of Christ changed everything. Thereafter, the old religions lost their fire. We can certainly love them for the beauty and wisdom that is in them but we should not return to them. Paganism is not equal to Christianity any more than the creation is equal to the Creator.

Extreme Times

We are living in very unusual times. As these times have been prepared for over a relatively long period, in terms of human life that is, we are less aware than we might be how very unusual these times are. Our relationship with both the material and spiritual worlds has changed dramatically. It would be fair to say that we now have no relationship with the spiritual world. It has receded further and further into the distance until for most people today it is way over the horizon. At the same time, we have become much more immersed in the material world. Our ability to control it has increased enormously but this, paradoxically, has reduced our awareness of what it actually is. We have made it more comfortable and removed many of its threats so are less able to see how unstable it can be and what an unnatural world the natural world is.

What do I mean by that? Obviously, the natural world is natural for us in a physical sense. But we are not just the body despite the relentless propaganda over the last couple of hundred years that has tried to persuade us that we are. Human beings are spiritual beings in material bodies which we have entered in order to learn the lessons that the material world exclusively offers. However, these lessons are spiritual in purpose, designed to enable us to unfold and express our divine potential. For those of us in any way aware of the soul, the physical world is a very constricted environment. Entering it is as though parts of our mind have been shut off while the external world is heavier, denser and deader than that we once knew and we sense this even if we have no clear memory of it. A Master once told me that the physical body '**was designed for beings of a lesser evolution than you and is more suited to their needs**'. These words would presumably apply to anyone who is aware of the greater reality beyond this physical band of the spectrum of being and they help explain why the material world can seem unnatural to many souls incarnated in it. Not only are we souls encased in bodies but even the bodies are cruder than they might be.

The Master's words also strike a blow right at the heart of the equality dogma. Lesser evolution? What kind of talk is this? We might accept evolution as a physical phenomenon though even there we normally stop short of allowing differences in terms of *Homo sapiens*, groups of which have been separated for tens of thousands of years. But spiritual evolution? If we accept that, we must recognise that human beings have souls and these souls are at different levels of development. That means some are more advanced than others. Equality would have to be completely reassessed. We could perhaps keep it as a description of our potential as spiritual beings but even there, who knows? It may be that some souls do have more potential to unfold divine being than others. There is nothing that says all souls must have equal potential. That is a pure supposition based on ideological beliefs. But, setting that aside and assuming all human souls do indeed have equal potential, they have certainly not all reached the same level of developing that potential.

One can see why this is a risky doctrine. The possibility of exploiting it to personal or societal advantage is there but that is no reason to disregard it. The perversion of a truth does not affect its status as truth. Ancient societies had the Mysteries in which more advanced souls were initiated into the secrets behind manifest life, and these were hidden partly to stop the unqualified gaining knowledge they could abuse. But Jesus Christ changed all that. He externalised the Mysteries and made them available to all. In actual fact, a soul still had to be spiritually qualified to avail itself of the full power of the revealed mystery but the opportunity was now there, potentially available to all. The truth was still protected because behind the outer form the inner mystery was only open to a soul to the degree that soul could comprehend it on the spiritual level. It remained inviolate, but the way to it had been opened up.

Ancient hierarchies, such as those of Egypt or India, were all spiritual hierarchies which is not surprising when you consider that the word means rule of the sacred. In these societies, which still retained a link to higher realities, the notion of souls being more or less evolved was understood. It was a basic truth and determined the way in which society was structured. Times have changed and the world has moved on to a very different view of human beings and their relationships to one another. This has certainly brought better understanding in certain areas. General consciousness has evolved and the old ways became outmoded, and yet the basic fact of human souls being at different levels of evolution remains. It should be noted that this does not specifically refer to intelligence. Intelligence is a part of it but the core of it is spiritual awareness. Intelligence can be a matter of brain function which is a material thing but spiritual evolution resides in the soul and manifests itself in ways which a materialistic society such as ours may not recognise.

How do souls become more or less evolved? To answer that fully one would have to go back to the very beginning of things and I am not qualified to do that. What can be said is that not all souls will have been created at the same time so some have been at the learning game a lot longer than others. There are waves of souls that come into being in different cycles. Some are simply a lot older than others. Then, some souls may have made greater progress than others. They have responded to experience better or else they have not been side-tracked so much by the glittering temptations of the phenomenal world. If souls are not equal even to begin with, which is perfectly possible, that too may be a factor. Perhaps not all souls in human bodies come from the same spiritual worlds. There are many dimensions of being and many souls come to the Earth to experience the possibilities that are offered here. Once incarnated they all have the same basic equipment, but the beings functioning in that equipment may be very diverse in their origins.

To say that there are souls at greater and lesser stages of evolution does not alter the fact that all are forms through which God is expressing himself and there is a unity in this respect. The disciples of equality have it right in that sense. But they mistake the inner for the outer, the ideal for the actual and the potential for the real. Oneness in God does not mean equality. It means that with every lifeform there are two factors to consider and both must be taken into account to see the creature as a whole. We might call these the being and becoming factors. In terms of being, we are all one. In terms of becoming, we are all different. Equality of being, variety of becoming. Don't confuse the two. You should not deny essential unity and nor should you deny essential difference. Spiritually, this is easy and natural and if you are operating from your spiritual self, you will do it automatically. It becomes a problem only when you operate from your intellectual self, and your thinking and being parts are divided as they generally are in the material self. Then you act according to an idea instead of whole-heartedly meaning as an undivided self.

As we have become more entrenched in the material world and lost what connection we had to the spiritual, our minds have changed. We have become more adept at technical thinking, the analytical, data-driven, measuring, controlling systemising ways of thought. These are behind the modern technocratic kinds of authority that wants to micro-manage everything and subject all human life to legislation and restriction. According to its own deluded mindset, this is for the general good but in reality it comes from two things. The denial of spirit and the desire for control. The latter is a front for the hunger for power and the former masks a hatred and fear of God. This way of thinking is thoroughly materialistic and is actually the foremost way in which evil manifests itself today. For what is evil but the rejection of God and the insistence that I can do better without him? Evil is fundamentally a spiritual thing. We are used to thinking of it in material terms but true evil may even appear good to one who denies God. It is adept at hiding itself even from itself. Of course, violence, murder, rape and so on are evils but they are evils of the body and there are evils of the soul too. Cold evils as opposed to hot ones, you might say. It is these we are often confronted with today. Evils of the soul are those which deny or downplay the reality of God and the spiritual purpose and destiny of the soul. This is the true good. Anything that works against the true good is evil so evil does not necessarily mean being nasty or even cruel as we see those things in a worldly sense. Some of the most evil people are highly moral in their own terms. If that statement shocks you, it means you do not understand the spiritual reality of good and evil.

In Tolkien's *Legendarium* Sauron started off as someone who simply wanted to improve life through complete control. How many modern technocrats might be said to fall into that category?

Because of the nature of the world today anyone serious about maintaining a contact with spiritual truth has to reject it. This has always been the case to a degree. The disciple has to deny the world meaning the worldly powers, its beliefs, ideologies and ways of thought and action. But today the situation has become critical as there is not even the semblance of divine recognition. Even religion is distinguished more by its social than its spiritual concerns with Christianity having in many respects become a branch of humanitarianism with some religion on the side.

That is why I am an extremist as, most probably, are you or anyone who retains a shred of real faith in a higher power and sees man's destiny as beyond this physical world. We are not really extremists in the sense that our position is bizarre, outlandish, unnatural or one-sided but we have been forced into apparent extremism because of the genuinely extreme nature of modern civilisation. It is the modern world that has adopted an extremist position of God-denying materialism. It is this world that has closed itself off from reality and lives in illusion. Anyone who holds fast to God and spiritual truth in such a situation necessarily becomes, by the standards of that world, an extremist.

Jesus was regarded by the religious and secular authorities of his time as an extremist. His disciples when they spread the word after his death were extremists. All the saints have been extremists even in the context of the religious societies in which they lived, and now when spiritual goodness and truth have been evicted from our lives and fakes and imitations are put up in their place anyone who affirms the inner reality of God will be condemned as a fanatic, an upstart, mad, even dangerous to societal stability and public order. Such a person is obliged to reject the fashionable ideas of the world. He must go against many perceived public values. In consequence, he will be branded a hater and perhaps, in some not too far off time, a criminal.

This situation has not happened by accident. We said at the beginning of this chapter that these times have been prepared for. It may appear that society has evolved in a certain direction over the last few hundred years because of science, education, secular progress etc., but actually we have been like sheep herded in a certain direction and we are now enclosed in the pen that was always waiting for us. Unfortunately, it was not the Good Shepherd who was doing the herding. The only way to understand our present predicament is to see it as the result of evil powers seeking to corrupt humanity and capture our souls. We have been fed half-truths and lies in order that our minds may conform to a certain shape for the demons who are behind the whole process (and no one can deny their skill)

147

know that we cannot be forced into rejecting God against our will. We can be lured into that sorry state but, when all is said and done, it must be our decision. They have set the trap and sweetened the bait but we have voluntarily walked into it with our eyes open. No one has to do this. Even if the path is opened up invitingly before us, we still have to set foot on that path and there is always a voice within to warn us against this if we will pay attention to it. If we don't listen to that voice that is because of a spiritual deficiency within us, hard as that may be to hear for anyone raised in the modern world. But don't blame the world. It inclines but does not compel.

As the world descends further into spiritual darkness it becomes more imperative for us to reject the whole edifice of materialistic atheism and not retain any aspect of it within our minds. There are today many people who protest against this or that aspect of modernity in its most up to date guise but who still accept the basic background premise of the materialistic ethos. However, it is becoming increasing meaningless to reject some of the consequences of materialism while still accepting the basic ideas that produced those things. The effects are in the cause. This does not mean a return to the past because mankind is meant to evolve and grow but once you acknowledge the reality of God and the spiritual path that puts everything else in a different perspective. We have built up a philosophy of life over the last three hundred years based on a totally wrong view of what a human being is. We need a radical reassessment. That means materialism does not just require pruning back to a more manageable state but must be completely uprooted and discarded. It is possible that it was a phase humanity had to go through to experience the consequences of the rejection of spirit but that phase should have come to an end some time ago. There are no benefits whatsoever at this late stage for maintaining a materialistic ethos in any shape, size or form.

Demons

This book is about the modern concept of equality and how it is part of a materialistic mindset that thinks in terms of measurement and number as opposed to the traditional spiritualised mode of consciousness which sees the world as a creation shot through with the spirit of the Creator who expresses himself in innumerable different ways, all of which are growing into greater life. Many of these ways would not be the direct expression of the Creator himself but come from other beings in the spiritual universe acting as sub-creators under God. All life is of God ultimately but the forms it takes may not be. God delegates.

If equality is a materialistic rather than spiritual idea, could we then say that the notion is simply a well-meaning but mistaken ideology? The motive behind it is to ensure justice and fairness for all and limit the exploitation of the less privileged by the more so. It may be wrong from a literal point of view but the intentions are good. Such might be the apparently reasonable claim and I don't doubt there is a large element of this present in the energy that drives the idea forwards. On the other hand, I am also sure that there is a substantial amount of envy and resentment involved in the process too. There is the desire to create society anew but there is also a desire to destroy and even a desire for vengeance, and it is because of these last two parts of the equation that the push for greater equality can be a means through which much evil can be accomplished.

It's really very simple. More equality means less quality. Greater emphasis on the horizontal axis means less on the vertical. Equality has been used and encouraged by dark powers to reframe society so that it no longer reaches up to spiritual levels. Everything high is being brought down. Everything must be, or seem to be, within reach of everybody. That means that there is nothing beyond this world or, if there is, it is so disfigured by being recontextualised to adapt to the image of the world that it becomes spiritually meaningless. The spiritual is not itself but made an aspect of the material.

This is not just an unfortunate side-effect of the drive towards greater justice. It is the deliberate steering of a particular intellectual ideology in a particular direction and it can be done because of the flawed nature of the ideology in the first place. That flaw simply has to be brought out and magnified but it was always present. You can see its presence right from the start but it has become the dominant theme over the last 50 years, and the process has picked up pace since around the turn of the millennium.

The aim of demons is spiritual corruption and for spiritual corruption to be effective it must be accepted as an act of choice. The fundamental law of self-conscious beings, which even God will not break, is free will. Everything is about choice. Do we want God and creation or do we want, or think we want, our own way or a way without God? It is the demons' desire to manipulate us into choosing the latter. Why, you might ask? As fallen beings who have exiled themselves from God they are motivated by a need to drag others down to share in their corrupted state. This is one simple psychological explanation. But there may be a practical one too. Having separated themselves from God they have cut themselves off from the source of life and it may be that to continue in existence they need, to put it bluntly, a food supply. In other words, the life energies of damned souls. We see earthly evil in terms of excessive desire for wealth and then for power. All that certainly exists and is driving much of the agenda today but behind it there is something else. The demons want spiritual power, power over souls which they can absorb into themselves. As I write this the image of Shelob, the spider in *The Lord of the Rings* comes to mind. This is a vivid depiction of demonic evil that wants to suck the life blood of its victims to sustain itself in its corrupt rottenness. A deeply unpleasant image, to be sure, but we need to face reality. However, let us recall that Shelob was banished by light, specifically, I believe, light from the stars or higher light. All evil is banished by spiritual light. This is our way forward. We have access to light through faith, prayer and visualisation. These are our weapons in the spiritual war. I was told by my teachers to imagine an armour of light around me that would protect me from evil influences when they attacked. This works.

The demons attack mankind in general, seeking to lead astray through false ideologies and beliefs. They want us to walk into a world of spiritual darkness thinking we are advancing towards a sunny tomorrow and an enlightened future. This is why they seek to depict dark as light and evil as good. No one, or hardly anyone, chooses evil knowing it to be evil but many will choose evil thinking it to be good, though such a choice can only be made by someone who has deadened spiritual sensitivity, denied God and is in the grip of some sin or other. We are all sinners, even the saints know that of themselves but what marks them out as saints is that they recognise and acknowledge their sinfulness. What makes a sinner a real sinner is the refusal to see himself as one.

The demons also attack on an individual level. My teachers told me that **'the greater progress you make, the more you will be assailed by evil in all its forms. Banish all evil thoughts and press on in love and faith'**. There are two points to draw from this. One, the spiritual aspirant is going to be attacked. You can think of this as a test. The attack will be where you are weak, through pride, laziness, fear, lust, whatever. It may not be recognised as such because the demons often work by blowing on dark embers already glowing in the heart or unhealthy ideas present in the mind. They stimulate and inflame, and it is up to you to be alert to this and stop the process going too far.

The second point concerns the solution to the problem. This takes us back to light dispelling darkness. **Banish all evil**

thoughts and press on in love and faith. You don't fight evil with evil. You fight it with good. If you feel yourself under attack, turn to God and allow his healing rays to drive out the darkness.

Evil does take different forms, as the Master says. There is the attack that seeks to draw you into sin, anger, hatred, resentment and such like, and here the evil may take no apparent form at all. Its aim is to convince you that this arises from within yourself. As indeed it may since evil powers can only work with what is already there, but it is fanned into greater activity by their doing. However, there is also a direct attack though this is fortunately rarer and here the aim may be not to corrupt but simply to steal light. I will give an example of one such incident in the hope that it may serve a useful purpose.

I apologise for touching on such an unpleasant subject but it's one the aspirant needs to be aware of as it may happen to him. Some time ago I experienced what appeared to be a psychic attack, and reflecting on it gave me a clue into what damnation might involve. The attack took place in the form of a dream, though it was like a waking dream in which you are neither completely asleep nor completely awake, and it consisted of a pair of incidents in which a sort of mind disintegration appeared to be attempted. It's possible that an extreme case of something similar could lie behind certain forms of possession and/or insanity, particularly if the victim was someone of a mediumistic nature already partially disabled by drug abuse or mental ill health.

Damnation is loss of the soul. Loss of the soul means loss of the self and a self is lost when it is disintegrated into existential chaos. The demons' work is destruction, the returning of cosmic order to the black pool of nothingness. This may be what damnation is. There are many forces in the modern world that aid and abet this disintegration, preparing the ground one might say, and some of them are happily pursued by foolish people because they give a kind of false ecstasy as the moorings of the mind are loosened and a horrible freedom is offered, freedom from the boundaries of order. In music we have rap, electronic dance or rave music, heavy metal and punk. These all dissolve structure into chaos in a more or less brutal fashion in which the rational mind is aggressively broken down to a sub-human instinctual maelstrom. The examples of modern art and literature follow a slightly different, possibly more cerebral, course but to the same end. Order into chaos. This can potentially be valid if a new and higher order is formed from the chaos but that is a rare, very rare, thing. Order does not arise naturally from chaos but requires the creative infusion of Logos to come to be, and this is certainly not happening with the examples I have cited. These are all to do with a sort of celebration of chaos. When you break boundaries there is an initial ecstasy as the freed energy flows out but it is soon dissipated and you have nothing left.

My experience was as follows. I had gone to bed around 11 o'clock but was unable to sleep as there was a lot of noise from party-goers outside. This put me in a fragile state, one in which normal psychic defences were weakened. I must have eventually got to sleep around 2 a.m. but it was disturbed and not restful sleep as I was still on edge. Then I had a very vivid dream. I dreamt the party-goers had come back with many other people and they were all outside laughing and shouting. I tried to put my head out of the window but it had been covered up with some material so I couldn't. Eventually I got the stuff off and put my head out to ask them to be quiet. The carousers were all skeletons which glowed a lurid green colour. They mocked me and made even more noise. Then they began attacking me psychically by which I mean they projected evil at me, some of which was expressed as this same lurid green in the form of 'dark light'. I can't describe it better than that. The psychic attack grew stronger so I prayed to Jesus for protection. But when I tried to banish them in the name of Jesus Christ,

I found I couldn't say the words. It was as though my brain had been saturated in a kind of heavy treacle which blocked it. I experienced a mental paralysis but eventually succeeded in pronouncing the words and found myself back in bed with them apparently gone.

But that wasn't the end of the dream/experience. While lying in bed I felt someone or something come in through the window with, of all things (go to work, Freudians), a supermarket trolley. This creature went through the room and downstairs where my two children sleep. I got up and followed it and found it outside their bedrooms with its trolley. I could clearly sense the aura of naked evil. It wasn't just bad. It was evil in a very pure way, dispassionate but absolute. Again, I tried to banish it using the name of Jesus and again, I couldn't get the words out. The thing began attacking me, not physically but on a spiritual level which I have known before and is very different as you feel as though something is trying to disintegrate your mind which will not function properly. Finally, I managed to call on the Masters and the thing was driven away. I knew I couldn't have dealt with it on my own. Then I woke up or returned to normal consciousness. I couldn't say which.

Now, a conventional psychologist would say that I had been disturbed by the noise outside and my over-stimulated mind made up this scenario as a result. I'm sure that had something to do with it but I am also convinced that is not all there is to it. I think the initial disturbed state created a kind of entry through which evil beings could attack. My defences were down. I am well aware most people would dismiss this as preposterous or else as evidence of mental derangement, even paranoia, but there was a very clear difference between this dream and the normal run of the mill sort, few of which I ever remember. This was more intense and vivid by several orders of magnitude. I was not particularly frightened because even in the dream world I find I can trust in God, but it was pretty hair-raising purely as an objective experience.

Demons

Assuming this was a psychic attack, I have to ask what its
purpose might have been and what it can teach us. That is the
reason I mention it here, and I return to the Masters' words
that all spiritual aspirants are attacked by evil as they progress.
This is because every person who breaks free of evil by turning
to God represents a nail in the coffin of evil, a step towards its
eventual destruction.

But why was it allowed? The powers of good can protect us up
to a point but if we are to become spiritually mature ourselves,
we have to learn to face evil. It exists. We must learn to deal
with it. And the way to deal with it is very simple and very
traditional. Call on Jesus Christ. You might find, as I did, that
something tries to stop you doing this. In my dream my brain
turned to mush but I called in my heart as well as my head and
I was answered. I also realised my utter dependence on God.
In your waking existence you can pretend this is not so but in
the vulnerable sleep state where you are exposed to the psychic
plane the room for self-deception and self-aggrandisement is
very much reduced. Everything is more raw and open.

I reflected on the things that attacked me and I came to the
conclusion that they were more like things than beings with
individual consciousness. The being in the second episode
particularly just seemed to be a kind of embodied malevolence.
After first appearing as a dark shadow, it took the form of an
old friend of mine but the eyes were pools of dead malice. It
may be that some demons are lost souls that have had their
individual selves hollowed out and become vessels for evil
in a ghastly parody of saints who can be vessels for God. The
saint has offered himself in love to God and God fills him with
himself. The lost soul has by his thoughts and behaviour given
himself to the devil but instead of being filled by goodness and
truth is taken over and used. It's as if the devil consumes them
and then operates through them though he can only do so to the
extent of their personal attainments of power, intelligence and

155

such like. It's horrible to think of but it may be a reality of the spiritual universe in which case we should be aware of it.

It occurs to me that what I have just described is precisely what the Nazgul are in *The Lord of the Rings*. Once again, Tolkien's spiritual instincts were true. The figure of Weston as described by C.S. Lewis in his novel *Perelandra*, an account of the temptation in the Garden of Eden transposed to Venus, is also to the point. Here we are shown a human soul that has been possessed by the devil and lost its humanity entirely. Weston has become a 'thing'. His soul has been taken over and its life energies absorbed by Satan. It was his resolute atheism that allowed this to happen.

There are many forces in the world today that are seeking to drive us towards spiritual dissolution, a dissolution that may possibly happen to those who have been sufficiently softened up in this life after they depart this life. I have spoken of certain forms of music and art. Drugs are another obvious example but there are also ideologies that seek to reduce everything to a uniform oneness. Shun these like, for they are of, the devil. Focus on the Good, the Beautiful and the True which are necessarily hierarchical and separative, two words which have been given a bad connotation today but simply mean not everything is equal which it could not be for absolute equality can only exist in nothingness. Always aspire upwards. Do not deny or dismiss the lesser for it too is of God but know that things are closer to or further away from him. They are not all at the same distance even though he dwells in all things.

Evil is running riot all over the world today but we should not pay it much attention. The manifestation of good conquers evil more effectively than actively fighting it. We should certainly be wise to evil but the more we focus on the good, the more we can help bring that out. I have written this chapter to point to the reality of demons for they are real but, I would like to end it by praising God who is the author of all good and who waits to welcome us into his kingdom if we will but accept the invitation.

Before I do conclude, though, I should draw attention to something which even those who do believe in the reality of demons sometimes miss. The aim of the demons is spiritual. They will use and spread materialism to separate us from God but they don't believe in it themselves. They know God exists. They have rejected him out of pride or ego or attachment to some particular sin which they have preferred to spiritual goodness but they know he exists. Their goal is to get human beings to reject God and that is why their purpose can often be better served in a world of peace and prosperity than one of deprivation and suffering. In the latter case people are more likely to turn to God whereas, *it is easier for a camel to go through the eye of a needle than for a rich man to get to heaven*. Most of us in the Western world, and increasingly the whole world, are rich now. We don't think we need God and therefore we happily do without him. In a societal collapse many individuals might turn to God as a last resort. This is why, although collapse does seem highly likely in the not too distant future, it is being staved off for the time being, the better to bring humans to the point at which they have denied God for so long that even disaster cannot move them to turn to him. It may sometimes seem strange that hope is one of the three primary virtues but it is precisely because it shows there is an active awareness of God present in the soul. Current demonic activity aims to erode that as much as possible before collapse is unleashed. So, make sure you never lose hope, whatever may take place in the outer world. Always put your faith in God who will never let you down if you do.

A Universe of Persons

1=1 and 2=2. But no number equals any other number unless qualified by something else. And in the realm of living things nothing equals anything else ever because living things are individual and therefore unique whatever form they take. Every animate being, and probably every inanimate object too because nothing is really inanimate, is either self-conscious or evolving towards self-consciousness or has moved beyond the limits of self-consciousness into divine union in which the individual self has become one with the Universal Self whilst losing nothing of its individuality which is only enhanced by the operation. All are totally unique. None are equal. The doctrine of equality rests and depends upon a mechanical universe of impersonal energies, a materialistic universe. But the universe does not derive from matter. It derives from spirit and spirit is personal. God is a Person and reality is comprised of beings whose fundamental and defining quality is personal. When all is said and done, everything is personal and this is why you have love. Without persons there could be no love. If we were all equal there could be a bland compassion but there could not be love for love is not equally directed to all. It is personal or it is not love. Jesus loved all his disciples but he did not love them all equally. He had his favourite, the beloved disciple John. Even the Buddha had a favourite disciple, his attendant Ananda.

Early man saw his environment as sacred. It was filled with, animated by, gods and spirits. Trees, rivers, the landscape, the elements, sun and moon, everything had a spiritual essence which was a being of some sort. We have moved a long way from that way of perceiving things because we have had to develop rational consciousness and personal freedom, neither of which we could have done while immersed in the world. We had to separate ourselves out from it in order to see ourselves.

But the fact remains that our early perceptions were true and perhaps it is now time to recapture the awareness of the whole world as a living being made up of other living beings, all of which operate together to create and sustain the natural world. This new awareness will not be the same as the old one because it will incorporate agency, the ability to engage actively with the world rather than just respond to it passively. In this way we fulfil our divine duty of co-creation with God. We were unconsciously one with life. We separated ourselves from life in order to develop the self. Now we need to acquire a conscious awareness of God while bringing to that the fruits of our individual development.

The pattern perceived by our ancestors in the natural world carries on into the spiritual regions. We have spoken of angels that function throughout the universe on all levels, and we have established that the organisation of life is hierarchical. Life is a ladder that stretches from Earth to Heaven. At the top suffusing all levels is God. His life pervades all life but each being on each level responds to that life and expresses it according to its own innate capacity, a capacity that is peculiar to that particular being but can also be further developed. To speak of equality shows a profound miscomprehension of what life is. It comes from the denial of soul and the reduction of all life to its material parts alone. This means that the intrinsic reality of the person is rejected. Personhood is not seen as a fundamental but an assemblage of component parts which give it an illusory appearance and which can be disassembled. In reality, a person is what we are and the rest comes from that. Within each soul there is God as the divine spark but what we are is the soul and each soul is whole and unique.

The soul is our individual self, the seed from which we develop, and as it grows from its originating point in the spiritual world it expands both upwards and downwards. It sends part of itself down into the material world to learn from experience in an externalised environment, meaning an environment in which subject and object become fully separated, and then it also expands upwards, stretching towards the light and pushing forth, as it were, branches from out of itself into higher planes and starting to become by these means conscious on those levels. In this sense the soul is like a tree, linking earth and sky.

The tree is an ancient and powerful spiritual symbol. At one time during the period of my instruction by the Masters I was told to **be like a tree**. In the context of my life then this related to simply being myself and not trying to force my opinions on anyone else, but the Masters' words were often capable of interpretation on several levels and I also understood them to be telling me that I should learn to be unmoved by the vicissitudes of emotion and stay grounded. And the image can be taken further. For example, a tree has a strong trunk with green leaves at the tips so it is both solid and delicate, firm and still at the centre but responsive and moving at its edges, a good example for the spiritual aspirant who must be centred in the unmoved Mover but able to respond to those around him. A tree gives – fruit, flowers, wood, oxygen – while seeming to ask little for itself. It stands tall but does not bend. It remains unbowed in the most difficult of circumstances. Its roots go deep down into the soil, the underworld even, while its branches extend to the heavens. Like the soul, it could be said to unite heaven and earth which is precisely what many mythologies have said it does do as the *axis mundi*. Then we have the Tree of Life, the Tree of Knowledge of Good and Evil, the Tree under which the Buddha gained enlightenment and the Tree on which Christ was crucified. The whole of manifestation is sometimes seen as a tree. It is the most profound of symbols.

But setting aside all that, I would like to consider the tree in a different aspect here, as a pattern for spiritual development. It is this aspect that I believe the Masters were referring to. One can certainly take the injunction in that respect.

So, how does the tree work in this way? To begin with, it is not a tower. There are many schools of esoteric and mystical practice, in both East and West, that try to reach God by building a tower to heaven. These have evolved a whole host of methods and techniques in the attempt to do this. It could be a form of yoga or mantras or particular meditations or work on the body or an elaborate metaphysical system or even drugs and sex. These all have their effects on consciousness but they do not bring true spiritual awareness because they are attempts to take heaven by force. In effect, to steal from God. They are man trying to gain the fruits of the spiritual on his own terms rather than God's and they will all eventually suffer the fate of that most famous tower, the Tower of Babel, if not in this life then later.

The path to true spiritual understanding and being is through growing not building. It should be a natural process that comes from within rather than being imposed from without and, in this context, all that comes from the mind is deemed the without because the thinking mind is external to spirit. That does not mean that growth cannot be encouraged. It should be but it should not be forced for then it will be artificial and therefore false.

Be like a tree means approach the spiritual path in an entirely natural way, always aspiring upwards but letting growth come from within and not trying to induce it by mechanical means. This ensures that the motive is right and comes from love of God rather than egotistic desire which seeks to gain the rewards of spirituality, power, consciousness, whatever, without being worthy of them. There are certain techniques that have been developed that may well bring results of a sort but those who build a tower in the attempt to gain heaven will eventually find it struck by a thunderbolt. This means they will sooner or later be brought back down to earth. The results of their seeking the spirit by building rather than growing will not last. The path to

God cannot be built by man because true spiritual opening only comes about through grace.

Grace is a concept that is lacking in many contemporary approaches to spirituality because so many of these dispense with God who is the source of grace. But Heaven can only be entered by means of grace, and grace is only bestowed on those who grow like trees. It never comes to those who build towers because these latter approach God on their terms rather than his.

Our theme is equality. Towers are like machines or things that can be built. They can be equal, one just the same as another. Trees are all different as things that grow are different. **Be like a tree** means be an individual and let your spiritual growth happen naturally. It will not happen without you willing it just as a tree aspires upwards to the light and will not grow when shut off from the sunlight, but it is not your personal will that can bring about growth. That can only render you open to growth and even then, it must be the pure aspiration of love not greedy, needy desire that drives the process onward.

Our perceived universe is just the outermost expression of a vast spiritual universe which extends throughout many planes of being. All these planes are populated by beings that have their natural home but can also move between them when required. Souls come to Earth to determine whether they are ready or fit to move to higher abodes. Here they are trained and tested, each according to its existing qualities. No soul is equal because none is the same. That does mean there are greater and lesser souls but all are included within the family of God. Let me leave the last words to the Masters. **Men are by no means equal on the earth plane but that is not a cause for dismissing anybody.**

Conclusion

The idea of equality might seem reasonable to someone who has no awareness of spiritual purpose or destiny and who does not appreciate that there is a world of greater reality behind this material world which gives our outer world whatever meaning it may have. But really it is an attempt to substitute a false and artificial good for truth. This may just seem a question of well-meaning people with good intentions making a mistake but the fact is the equality idea has been used for several decades as a tool to chip away at spiritual truth and reduce the higher to the level of the lower, creating a kind of inverted hierarchy in the process. And the well-meaning people cannot be exonerated either because they are guilty of a lack of orientation to spiritual truth. Some may even wish to supplant that with their own version of reality.

Equality exists nowhere in nature. Creation itself could only happen when the darkness of non-manifestation was shattered by light resulting in the first and fundamental inequality which then became the ground on which cosmic order was built. Creation depends on separation and difference. An unqualified equality would have kept the universe in darkness.

And darkness is what those who promote equality would have us return to for equality can only truly exist at ground level, when everything has been brought down to nothing. If anything is to be it must be something and no one thing is like any other thing. Light has an infinite range of shades. Darkness is just darkness. There is true equality only in darkness.

But if nature and the universe are both formed on the principle of inequality could equality still be something that human beings should aspire to and work towards while recognising that it may not ever be literally possible to achieve? First of all, why would you wish to pattern human evolution on something that does not exist in spiritual or natural terms? Are you not thereby working against the flow of life, setting yourself up against reality? But secondly, there is no need for this. For with the principle of inequality goes that of responsible hierarchy which means that everything has its proper place in what used to be known as the Great Chain of Existence which is the basis of cosmic order. Allowing and enabling all human beings to develop themselves in the context of what they are is absolutely what we should be doing but this has nothing to do with equality which is a chimera, the pursuit of which will only disrupt the order and harmony on which the universe is based. This is not the same as saying everyone should know and keep to their place because another principle of life is growth. But again this has nothing to do with equality. This idea simply introduces a false perspective.

Look at history and you will see that the notion of equality appears in civilisations only in their dying days when their creative energies are burning out. That does not in itself make it bad or wrong but it does indicate that it is part of the decadent phase of any particular culture which arises when that culture has lost connection to deeper realities and contents itself with wholly secular concerns. It comes about in a declining phase not a developing one.

Western civilisation is dying. At its peak it scaled great heights but it has fallen a long way down since then because of its denial of spirit. Unfortunately, most people think of this as an advance and a liberation from superstition because this denial freed us to explore and exploit the material world to a greater degree, but the initial burst of energy that came from that is rapidly dissipating. Actual progress is starting to slow down and a lot of what we thought of as progress turns out to be not without problems. Even our increased recognition of the horrors of violence and war can be understood as a greater fixation on the physical self and material well-being.

How can anyone live without acknowledging God? Within each human soul there is the divine stamp that is our life and the core of our being. How can we ignore this? But it seems millions of people do. What is going on inside these people that they have closed themselves off to such a degree from reality and all that makes life worthwhile? There is no doubt that the material world has solidified so that the connection to spirit is much harder to make but still it is there. There is also no doubt that demonic powers have attacked on numerous fronts to make us believe the material world is all there is but we don't have to succumb to their lies. Even if everyone around us prefers darkness to light we do have the light within us and we can respond to that if we are spiritually responsible and true children of our Father.

Perhaps that's it. Most people don't care about God because they care too much about themselves. They are too fixated on their worldly hopes and ambitions and their personal desires. They are too identified with their bodies or their feelings or their thoughts and so never look more deeply within themselves. Then there are those who are too attached to a particular sin to be willing to acknowledge that it is a sin which they would have to do if they recognised God. Such people are setting themselves up to be the victims of the dark powers to whose influence they will become more and more susceptible.

We are unable to perceive the inner workings of spiritual evil because we don't acknowledge spiritual good. This makes us easy to manipulate and deceive and lead astray. An essential task for all human beings today is to recognise that the source of evil is hidden. It does not come from this material world. It actually emanates from powerful beings on the spiritual plane working through their emissaries at lower levels and in this world. Those regarded as evil in the material world are merely pawns of these higher beings who are the principalities and powers spoken of by St Paul in his letter to the Ephesians (6:12).

These demons think in the long term. They have prepared for this time over many centuries and when we look back, we can see the gradual turning of the screw, how one thing, relatively innocent in itself, led to another which led to another and so on. But there was only ever one direction. This should show us that mortal men alone cannot be responsible for the plan of spiritual destruction even if they are indirectly responsible for enacting many of its stages.

Does this sound sensationalist? That thought again might come to mind as a result of seeds sown by evil powers over many years. They function best when unrecognised or downgraded to cartoon characters or softened by being fictionalised. In the public mind the teeth of supernatural evil have been drawn by its regular appearance in film and on TV. It can be dismissed as entertainment or deriving from fantasy and fiction. This is not without some advantages though. When you have a writer such as Tolkien, who was very aware of the reality of supernatural evil, you have a powerful depiction of its reality and how it operates and then your mind is primed to recognise it later on when you begin to wake up.

People don't believe in God because there is no proof but you cannot prove spiritual realities by material means. Expand your horizons beyond the material world and you will find proof. But this will not be intellectual proof. Spirit cannot be proven by the intellect or the mind as normally considered. It can only be known. This is why faith is important. Faith is not just belief but the opening up of the mind to wider vistas. It is like being in a dark room with the curtains drawn. Faith is opening a window through which daylight can stream in.

It is possible that as the limitations of the materialistic worldview become more apparent to more people there will be a reaction. This has already happened to a limited extent, beginning in the 1960s though the movement seemed to lose energy around the turn of the millennium. But as material privations start to manifest themselves, as it is very likely they are about to do, it may happen again and this time to a larger degree. This is when we have to be ready to warn people that not all that seems spiritual is good. At the end of the Roman Empire mystical and occult sects flourished but these were mostly degenerate remains of the ancient mystery religions with an emphasis more on the psychic than the spiritual. They were demon infested and only cleaned up by the purity of the vital Christian force that also spread at that time. This phenomenon could recur. The demons will have prepared a spiritual movement that will bestow mystical experiences of a sort and also increase the lower psychic powers thus exposing their possessors to a false spiritual plane. We need to be rightly motivated, which means searching for God rather than spiritual pyrotechnics, to avoid falling into this trap. As was the case almost 2,000 years ago, the key will be our acceptance or otherwise of Christ.

The subtitle of this book is Reclaiming the Soul. It is the soul, the spiritual component of our being, that is denied when equality is asserted for each soul when created is original and unique, and its experiences bring out its individuality further. If you believe in the soul, you cannot also believe in equality. To do so is to apply quantitative principles to a realm of quality.

A world of real equality would be a world with no room for improvement. It would be flat, without height or depth and nothing to aspire towards. It would lack the vertical dimension and the sense of beyond. It would be a world in which numbers and measurement really were at the root of being and that would be a controllable world in which there was neither freedom nor mystery. Numbers relate to the functioning of the material world in its material aspects and they obviously have their place in the structuring of that world. They provide knowledge of how it works and reveal certain properties of material things. But they cannot tell us anything about what lies behind the material world or its source or how the life and consciousness that appear in it come to be. Numbers can tell us about the form of things but they tell us nothing about what these things are in themselves.

If you rely on number to tell you about the world, you kill the world. You reduce it to a machine and you reduce human beings to machines, dead things even if they move about and talk. The fact is that numbers only relate to the shape and pattern of living beings. They cannot describe or reveal anything about the inner life and essence of beings, their true nature, their spiritual reality, what they actually are. The world of the mathematicians is a true world but it only relates to externals and appearance. God may be a Geometer in terms of his outer activities but in himself, in his spiritual essence, he is a deep mystery that the quantitative science of numbers cannot begin to understand. When you reduce life to numbers, the individual becomes just a number itself, a mere unit. Then it has no autonomy but must fit into the mathematical structures on which society is run. It is just a statistic and its personal integrity has gone. Genuine equality would, could, only exist in such a world but it would be a world without spirit.

Fortunately for us the world is not like that. It has its numerical, quantitative side but that relates to matter only. There is a spiritual side too and that is primary. You, you who read these lines, have complete spiritual reality as a person, an authentic unique individual which cannot be reduced to anything else for it is whole in itself. In a universe of individuals there can be no equality but there can be love. Which would you rather have, equality or love? You can't have both.

About the Author

William Wildblood was born in London. After a period working as an antiques dealer, he left the UK to run a guesthouse in South India. He later moved to France where he was an occasional guide at the medieval abbey of le Mont Saint-Michel. He returned to England at the end of the twentieth century, working for various magazines including seven years as an antiques columnist. He has written several other books including *Meeting the Masters, Remember the Creator* and *Earth Is a School*. *The Spiritual Crisis of Modern Man* is a collection of his online writings and he also contributed to *Albion Awakening* with John Fitzgerald.

AXIS MUNDI
BOOKS

EXPLORING THE WORLD OF HIDDEN KNOWLEDGE

Axis Mundi Books provide the most revealing and coherent explorations and investigations of the world of hidden or forbidden knowledge. Take a fascinating journey into the realm of Esoteric Mysteries, High Magic (non-pagan), Mysticism, Mystical Worlds, Goddess, Angels, Aliens, Archetypes, Cosmology, Alchemy, Gnosticism, Theosophy, Kabbalah, Secret Societies and Religions, Symbolism, Quantum Theory, Conspiracy Theories, Apocalyptic Mythology, Unexplained Phenomena, Holy Grail and Alternative Views of Mainstream Religion.
If you have enjoyed this book, why not tell other readers by posting a review on your preferred book site? Recent bestsellers from Axis Mundi Books are:

On Dragonfly Wings
A Skeptic's Journey to Mediumship
Daniela I. Norris
Daniela Norris, former diplomat and atheist, discovers communication with the other side following the sudden death of her younger brother.
Paperback: 978-1-78279-512-4 ebook: 978-1-78279-511-7

Inner Light
The Self-Realization via the Western Esoteric Tradition
P.T. Mistlberger
A comprehensive course in spiritual development using the
powerful teachings of the Western esoteric tradition.
Paperback: 978-1-84694-610-3 ebook: 978-1-78279-625-1

The Seeker's Guide to Harry Potter
Dr Geo Trevarthen
An in-depth analysis of the mythological symbols and themes
encountered in the Harry Potter series, revealing layers of
meaning beneath the surface of J K Rowling's stories.
Paperback: 978-1-84694-093-4 ebook: 978-1-84694-649-3

The 7 Mysteries
Your Journey from Matter to Spirit
Grahame Martin
By simply reading this book you embark on a journey of
transformation from the world of matter into spirit.
Paperback: 978-1-84694-364-5

Angel Healing & Alchemy
How To Begin Melchisadec, Sacred Seven & the Violet Ray
Angela McGerr
Angelic Healing for physical and spiritual harmony.
Paperback: 978-1-78279-742-5 ebook: 978-1-78279-337-3

Colin Wilson's 'Occult Trilogy'
A Guide for Students
Colin Stanley
An essential guide to Colin Wilson's major writings on
the occult.
Paperback: 978-1-84694-706-3 ebook: 978-1-84694-679-0

The Heart of the Hereafter
Love Stories from the End of Life
Marcia Brennan
This book can change not only how we view the end of
life, but how we view life itself and the many types of love
we experience.
Paperback: 978-1-78279-528-5 ebook: 978-1-78279-527-8

Kabbalah Made Easy
Maggy Whitehouse
A down to earth, no-red-strings-attached look at the mystical
tradition made famous by the Kabbalah Center.
Paperback: 978-1-84694-544-1 ebook: 978-1-84694-890-9

The Whole Elephant Revealed
Insights Into the Existence and Operation of Universal Laws
and the Golden Ratio
Marja de Vries
An exploration of the universal laws which make up the
dynamic harmony and balance of the universe.
Paperback: 978-1-78099-042-2 ebook: 978-1-78099-043-9

Readers of ebooks can buy or view any of these bestsellers by
clicking on the live link in the title. Most titles are published
in paperback and as an ebook. Paperbacks are available in
traditional bookshops. Both print and ebook formats are available
online. Find more titles and sign up to our readers' newsletter at
http://www.johnhuntpublishing.com/mind-body-spirit
Follow us on Facebook at htt ps://www.facebook.com/OBooks
and Twitter at https://twitter.com/obooks